Love and Logic®
Powder Room Reader

JIM FAY & CHARLES FAY, PH.D.

Love and Logic®
Powder Room Reader

JIM FAY & CHARLES FAY, PH.D.

Love and Logic®
INSTITUTE, Inc.
800-338-4065 · www.loveandlogic.com

Love and Logic Institute, Inc.
2207 Jackson Street, Golden, CO 80401-2300
www.loveandlogic.com
800-338-4065

LOVE AND LOGIC, LOVE & LOGIC, BECOMING A LOVE AND LOGIC PARENT,
AMERICA'S PARENTING EXPERTS, LOVE AND LOGIC MAGIC, 9 ESSENTIAL SKILLS
FOR THE LOVE AND LOGIC CLASSROOM, EARLY CHILDHOOD PARENTING
MADE FUN, and 🔒 are registered trademarks or trademarks of the Institute For
Professional Development, Ltd. and may not be used without written permission expressly
granted from the Institute For Professional Development, Ltd.

Library of Congress Cataloging-in-Publication Data

Fay, Jim.
  Love and logic powder room reader / Jim Fay & Charles Fay.
    p. cm.
  ISBN 978-1-935326-05-2
  1. Child rearing. 2. Parent and child. 3. Parenting. 4. Manipulative behavior in children. 5.
Communication in families. I. Fay, Charles, 1964- II. Title.
  HQ769.F28225 2009
  649'.1--dc22
                        2009050529

Cover & Interior Design by Michael C. Snell, Shade of the Cottonwood, Lawrence, KS
Indexing by Dianne Nelson, Shadow Canyon Graphics, Golden, CO
Project Coordinator: Kelly Borden

Published and printed in the United States of America

Table of Contents

CHAPTER ONE

Early Childhood

Save Most of Your Words for Happy Times
Dr. Charles Fay

What's the best way to make an otherwise effective technique backfire? It's simple: Talk too much.

In the store, I recently witnessed an unusually upset toddler whining to his mother about how "mean" she was and how badly he "needed" the toy she was telling him to put back on the shelf. This well-meaning mother quickly jumped into "psychotherapy mode" by listing all of the reasons why her three year old didn't need the toy, how it might put his eye out, how he might get one next year, why he shouldn't be so upset, how sorry she was that he couldn't have it, that money doesn't grow on trees, etc.

There they were—both of them—on their knees.

While well meaning, this mother was actually feeding the fire by talking way too much! There exists a basic rule about doing discipline with kids of all ages:

The more words we use when our kids are acting up, the LESS effective we become.

Save most of your words for happy times.

Thanks for reading!

The Power of the Silent Voice
By Jim Fay

"Little Teddy is ruining our class," moaned the preschool teacher. "I think he is going to need some intense therapy. Nothing we do works to settle him down. I'd like to use the UH-OH SONG with him, but I don't want to bring any more attention to him."

One wise old teacher made a suggestion that the staff use the UH-OH SONG without the words. "Each time he acts out, take him quietly by the hand and lead him silently to the recovery chair. Leave him there without one word. If he leaves the chair, calmly and silently take him back as many times as necessary. Whatever you do, don't say a single word," she suggested.

This experiment worked like dynamite. Within a few days Teddy had calmed down and the class was back to normal.

Many parents have found this technique to be very successful in their homes. Is it worth an experiment?

....

The Power of Joyful Modeling
Dr. Charles Fay

Anyone who knows little kids knows that they want to be "big" like their parents. Great parents take advantage of this by making a big deal out of modeling the things they want their little ones to do.

To soup up this strategy, smart parents also express as much joy as possible as they are modeling.

One wise daddy said, "Instead of telling my three year old to brush her teeth, I just jump up from the table after a meal and say, 'Wow! I can't wait to brush my teeth!' Then I run into the bathroom and make a bunch of noise so that she hears how much fun I'm having. In a minute or two, she's tugging on me, demanding her toothbrush!"

When little ones see us having lots of fun doing things, they don't want to be left out. While it can be frustrating when a toddler wants to "help" us dust, wash dishes, fold clothes, and complete other chores, the dividends of being patient are priceless.

Might it be smart to list all of the things you want your kids to do when they are teens and make a habit of joyfully modeling these things when they are toddlers?

Thanks for reading!

....

Don't Let Your Baby "Cry it out"
Dr. Charles Fay

There's nothing more important during the first two years of a child's life than feeling the love and comfort of one's parents!

Some folks worry about "spoiling" their babies. They think, "If we hold her too much she'll be needy."

Others fret, "He'll never learn how to calm himself down if we comfort him too much when he cries."

Some even argue, "Well, he's just trying to get his way when he cries."

THESE ARE MYTHS!

It's impossible to spoil babies by holding them too much, comforting them when they cry, or giving them too much attention.

This nurturing and love teaches us to nurture and love. As a result, we feel bad when we act badly. We have a strong conscience that guides our way.

What's our advice for parenting tots younger than two? Smile at them as much as possible, comfort them when they cry, hold them with loving arms, whisper sweet stuff in their ears, and let them see how much fun you're having.

As they begin to need more limits, you'll begin to see a child who loves you too much to rebel with much force.

Thanks for reading!

....

Three Steps for Little Tykes
Dr. Charles Fay

Over the past three decades, we've noticed that the most successful parents begin early in their children's lives with these steps:

Step One: Pray for your teeny-tiny ones to misbehave or be resistant. Remember: The road to wisdom is paved with mistakes.

Step Two: Sing a sweet, empathetic, "Uh oh!"

Step Three: Follow through by taking over in a loving way.

Little Larry is nine months old and ready to do some major crawling and some major grabbing of Fluffy the cat's tail. Since his parents are praying for misbehavior, they are elated instead of exasperated.

They sing, "Uh Oh," and put Larry into his playpen away from Fluffy.

Larry is now sixteen months old. He's being resistant to getting into his car safety seat. His mother's prayers have been answered!

"Uh oh," she sings as she straps him into his car seat.

Larry is now three. Every time he hears, "Uh oh," he thinks, "Uh oh!" and stops misbehaving.

It's never too early to teach your children that your word is gold. Thanks for reading!

....

"I Don't Care"
Jim Fay

Lisa was just about at the end of her patience with little Freddie. He was at that age where he was testing her constantly, and now he was at it again. He had been told many times not to tease the cat. In fact, she had threatened all sorts of dire consequences if he did. But alas, here he was teasing the cat in spite of her warnings and threats.

It was at this point that she finally realized that threats and warnings are a waste of time. She would have to take action with the Love and Logic® "Uh, Oh Song."

She whisked Freddie off to his room and told him that she would see him when he was sweet. In the true tradition of the strong-willed child, Freddie didn't cry or whine, he shouted through the door, "I don't care. I like it when I have to stay in my room! So there!"

Stymied for a moment, Lisa remembered a line from her Love and Logic book and shouted through the door, "That's great, Sweetie. Now we're both happy."

As she proudly walked away, she thought to herself. "This is great. No anger, no lecture, no threats, and I think I'm going to use that line many times before he's grown."

Training for Shopping
Jim Fay

When Dan was little and went shopping with his mom, the words he heard most were "Don't touch!" When he became a dad and went shopping with his kids, the words he said most were "Don't touch!" It was frustrating to shop with his kids. They wanted to touch everything. That's what they see the big people doing. Thinking there had to be a better way, he decided to conduct some training.

"Guys, here's how I know what I can touch in the store. I know that packaged things probably won't break. I can touch them. Things that are not packaged get broken easily. So I look at the price tag and see if I have enough money to pay for it if it gets broken.

From now on you can do the same thing. Feel free to touch anything if you have enough money saved up to pay for it."

Now the words he hears most in the store are, "Dad. Can I afford to pay for this?" A little time in training goes a long way toward happier parenting.

It's Never Too Early to Start Teaching Responsibility
Dr. Charles Fay

There's good news! As soon as a child is old enough to spit pureed peas, they are old enough to start learning responsibility.

Little kids learn about responsibility from three steps:

- Being naughty
- Seeing us being sad for them
- Experiencing a bit of inconvenience, boredom, or slight discomfort as a result of their poor behavior

When a teeny, tiny tyke spits peas, they learn responsibility by hearing us sing "Uh oh" and by being placed gently in their crib for a little "calm down time."

When a little one crawls away when we are trying to change them, they learn by hearing us say, "Uh oh" and being gently held in place until they relax and comply.

When our little sweeties toss their bottles off the highchair, they learn by hearing us say, "Uh Oh" and seeing their bottles go back in the refrigerator.

Wise parents know that teaching responsibility during the first two years is a lot easier than teaching it during the teen years.

Thanks for reading!

....

The Perfect Gift – A Box
Jim Fay

Can little kids develop imaginations despite overindulgent parents? Thankfully, yes. Just watch them open a gift and have more fun playing with the box than the toy that was inside.

I was at my friend's house and noticed her son's "play room." There was every possible toy and gadget in that room. All I could say to myself was, "This poor kid, he'll never be happy." How could this little guy ever learn to use his imagination when the toys do all the work?

Then I noticed him digging a hole in the backyard with an old hand shovel of his mothers as he made engine noises. He had made his own construction site and was building a great city. And then I said to myself, "Thank heavens, some kids have imaginations in spite of their parents' overindulgence."

Don't take a chance; your kid might not be as lucky as this little guy.

The Cause and Effect of Cuddles and Kisses
Jim Fay

I was in the mall with my wife, Shirley, and noticed a wonderful loving smile on her face. I know that smile; it's the one she always gets when she sees a tiny baby.

This little guy looked like he was about a month old. He was not happy, and he was letting everyone in the mall know that he was not happy. We all recognize the cry of really young babies— piercing!

He was with his very young-looking daddy. Dad may have been young, but he knew exactly what to do. He took the little guy out of his stroller, smiled at him, comforted him, gave him a soft kiss, and cuddled him. And before we knew it the crying stopped.

During the first year of life children are a bundle of basic needs. They cry to get these needs met. Later on it becomes more confusing for parents because children have both needs and wants. At this time it becomes important for them to learn about delayed gratification. Wise parents let their kids wait a little longer to get their needs met, and they are very selective about fulfilling their wants.

Taming Toy Aisle Tantrums
Dr. Charles Fay

Listed below are some tantrum-taming tips:

Remember that these tips won't work if we don't use empathy.
Empathy allows us to discipline our kids without losing their love.

Keep moving.
When your kids begin to beg, do not stop! The quicker you move, the fewer tantrums they will have.

When appropriate, allow your child to learn that stuff costs money.
Some Love and Logic parents say, "You may have that as long as you can pay for it before we leave." Then they say to the checkout clerk, "My son wants this item, but I'm not sure he has the money. I'll let you two work it out. I'll be waiting over there."

Allow your kids to learn by saving some money and making some purchases.
When is it best for kids to learn that it's unwise to blow all of their money on something that will soon break or become boring? As early in life as possible!

When tantrums erupt, don't be afraid to use some gentle humor.
"Oh sweetie. That's a good fit, but your last one was better," often works magic to take the fury out of fits.

Thanks for reading!

Practice Morning Sessions
Dr. Charles Fay

Have you noticed how slow little kids move when we are in a hurry to get to work?

We can learn a great deal from successful preschool and kindergarten teachers. Observing them at work, we see them practicing with their students just about every behavior or routine required for the smooth operation of a school.

Listed below are some tips for practicing mornings with your kids:

Tip #1: **Practice when you are not in a hurry.**
A good time is often Saturday or Sunday afternoon.

Tip #2: **Make it a fun game of "pretend."**
Some parents say, "Let's be silly! Go pretend to be sleeping, and I will come and wake you up! Then we can see who can get ready the fastest."

Tip #3: **Help your kids make a visual checklist by taking pictures of them getting dressed, eating, brushing their teeth, etc.**
Note: If you don't have a camera, your kids can help you make some drawings.

Tip #4: **Put the pictures in order and post them on the refrigerator, wall, bathroom mirror, etc.**

Tip #5: **Above all else, have fun!**
The more fun you have doing this, the more your little ones will learn.

Thanks for reading!

A Reminder About Reminders
Dr. Charles Fay

It's humbling. Parenting, that is. Is it just me, or do you also find yourself slowly forgetting to use your skills?

I was reminded to use mine by a mother and her sweet yet sassy toddler. There they sat—right behind me on the airplane. When the seatbelt sign illuminated, Mom reminded her daughter no less than twelve times to buckle up.

Honestly, I wasn't trying to be nosey. Neither were the other seventy-five or so passengers who overheard the exchange. It's just that the volume went up with each reminder provided.

It was obvious that this mother loved her daughter deeply. But, very sadly, she was training her child to need at least eleven reminders before complying. Can you imagine the teen years if things don't change around that home?

We have the power to do better by our kids! How? By remembering to set the limit once... and follow through without anger, threats, or repeated reminders.

The flight would have been a much happier one if Mom had told her little sweetie once, and then buckled the seat belt for her if she didn't comply.

Thanks for reading!

··

Why Childhood Fits Are Fantastic
Dr. Charles Fay

Fits are great! Yep! Despite popular parental opinion, childhood fits are fantastic.

Too frequently we hear things like, "I couldn't do that! She'd throw a fit!" or "That Love and Logic doesn't work. When we tried it, he got really mad!"

Some of the worst behaved kids (and adults) grow up in homes where their parents bend over backwards to make sure that they are never inconvenienced, bored, disappointed, or upset in any way. What such well-meaning parents fail to understand is that they are just postponing their children's fits until less opportune times.

After studying families for decades, we at Love and Logic believe that all children are born with a set allotment of fits that must be used up within their lifetime. As you know, some tykes are born with far more fits than others! When fits aren't used up during childhood, they get postponed for later. Do you know an adult who probably didn't have enough fits when they were a child?

When is it best for our children to use up most of their fits? When they are smaller than us or bigger than us? The next time your child has a fit over your loving use of Love and Logic, you might say to yourself, "Yes! That's one more fit he won't have to throw when he's bigger than me!"

Thanks for reading!

It's a Great Time to Donate Those Older Toys!
Dr. Charles Fay

The holidays are wrapping up and, chances are, your kids have a whole bunch of older toys they're no longer interested in. By involving our kids in selecting and packing up the toys they'd like to donate, and taking the toys to a local church, synagogue, shelter, etc., we do good for the world and good for our kids. Get the process started in a brief and simple way:

> *You got some really nice things for Christmas this year, sweetie. How nice! Do you know there are a lot of kids who aren't so lucky? Let's pick some of your old toys and give them to kids who don't have any.*

Some children suddenly want to keep ALL their old toys when they hear this. Just reassure them that you won't be taking the toys they love and play with the most—only the ones that gather dust.

11

It never hurts to add one more thing:

I have some things that I don't use anymore, so I'm going to give them away, too.

Thanks for reading!

....

Basic Love and Logic for Very Young Children
Dr. Charles Fay

How early in a child's life can we start using Love and Logic?

As soon as they can spit their pureed food, crawl away from you when you are changing their diaper, etc. Fortunately, the basic process is very simple:

Step one: **Pray for misbehavior.**
Mistakes made early in life have far more affordable consequences than those made later.

Step two: **Sing an empathetic, "Uh oh."**
The fewer words we use when our kids are acting up, the more successful we will be.

Step three: **Provide a loving consequence.**
There exist only three basic consequences for small children:
• Change your location by walking away and paying no attention to them
• Change the location of the problem object by taking it away
• Change the child's location by carrying them to their room, buckling them into their stroller, etc.

Step four: **Repeat as needed.**
When parents repeat this basic process with great consistency, they find that they only get to the second step most of the time. Quite quickly, their tots learn that "Uh oh" means that it's wise to start acting sweet!

Thanks for reading!

Teaching Happiness
Dr. Charles Fay

I think it's safe to say that all of us want our kids to be happy and to become happy and productive adults. One way to up the odds involves modeling happiness. Another fairly obvious piece of the puzzle is teaching kids to be responsible. A less obvious, yet equally critical, piece involves the types of behaviors and emotions that receive the most attention in our homes. Let's consider Larry and Louise:

> *By the time little Larry is three years old, he's already learned that his parents spend more time talking to him when he is upset than when he's happy.*
>
> *By the time little Louise is three, she's learned that her parents spend more time talking to her when she's happy than when she is upset.*
>
> *Larry's well-meaning parents aren't aware that they are actually rewarding and reinforcing sadness and misery.*
>
> *While Louise's parents nurture her when she is hurting, they are careful to avoid sending the message that being upset is the best way to get what you want in life.*

I bet you can predict which child will have the happiest life.

Who Might be Listening?
By Jim Fay

Six-year-old Paul was at the family reunion when he asked his uncle if he could see the moths in his billfold.

"What do you mean?" asked Uncle Fred.

"My dad told my mom that you were so tight that if you ever opened your billfold, moths would fly out, and I want to watch," replied Paul.

We all know where Paul picked this up. Kids remember all the things they hear through eavesdropping, while they often don't listen well to the things they are told directly.

Unfortunately, Paul has another problem. He has overheard his parents criticizing his teachers and the school. That could be the reason he believes that his bad grades are not the result of laziness, but because he doesn't have to do what the stupid teacher says.

Regardless of how we feel about the school or the teacher, it is real bad business to say it where our kids can overhear it. Better we send a consistent message that achievement comes through hard work and listening to the teachers.

Study the DVD, "Hope for Underachieving Kids" to get practical techniques for helping your kids become top students.

TV? None During the Early Years.
By Jim Fay

Want to hear a really scary thought? Here is a quote from the *New York Times*:

> "On a typical day, 61 percent of babies one-year or younger watch TV or videos, with average viewing of more than an hour [the study found]. A third of children under 6 have a TV in their bedroom. And more than half of parents surveyed said their main reason for putting a TV in their child's room was so that they or other family members could watch their own shows."

Is the real purpose of television to reduce the amount of time we spend interacting, playing, exploring, and talking with our kids? I know of no research that tells us any good can come of this.

Companies are now marketing videos that are supposed to be good for infants. Don't fall for this advertising.

As our children's brains develop, each moment of face-to-face interaction is precious, as it stimulates a growing brain in a positive way. Television bombards the brain with fast-moving visual images that addict the brain to stimulation while putting your baby's future at risk for:

- Attention problems
- Concentration problems
- Lowered academic performance
- Motivation problems

Is using TV as a babysitter worth the gamble?

Baby Parenting
Dr. Charles Fay

About nine months ago, my wife and I were blessed with a wonderful little bundle of joy baby boy! Since our other kiddos are ages 14 and 22 years, we're re-learning a lot about babies. We're also being given a lot of advice about how to proceed, as well as plenty of books on the subject.

Some books say, "Don't hold them too much! They'll get spoiled."

Other books say, "Make sure they're fed on a tight time schedule. Make them wait until it's time for a feeding."

Some of our friends say, "Just let him cry it out at night until he falls asleep."

Fortunately, I was blessed with the opportunity to spend eleven years of my life learning from the scientific research on child development. From this blessing, I can say without any reservation that the advice mentioned above is dead wrong.

15

In a nutshell, here's what research really says about parenting during the first year of life:

Love them and take good care of them. Comfort them when they cry. Feed them when they are hungry. Hold them as often as you can. Don't worry for a moment about spoiling them by giving them too much attention.

In our Early Childhood Package, we teach that the first year of life is all about bonding and attachment. As the second year looms closer, parents find more and more opportunities to set and enforce limits. The more practical tools we have for doing both, the more successful we will be!

Thanks for reading!

....

How Early Can We Start?

Dr. Charles Fay

Many people ask, "How early in our child's life can we start using Love and Logic?"

"As soon as they can crawl over and grab something they aren't supposed to have," is typically my answer.

Generally speaking, most little ones begin to crawl around and test limits anywhere between six and eight months of age. This is the prime time to begin teaching them two things:

• That you love them enough to set limits
• That you are willing to consistently enforce the limits you set

Here's what it looks like: Sweet little Sara crawls over to the table, pulls herself up, and starts grabbing for her mommy's coffee mug, the remote control, or some other forbidden item. In a loving yet firm tone, Mommy sings, "Uh Oh!" and gently picks Sara up, placing her in her playpen, highchair, or some other spot that's safe.

Mommy knows that the fewer words and less attention she provides at this time, the quicker Sara will learn.

Sara doesn't need to be in there long at this age! All it takes is just three or four minutes for her to miss being able to crawl around and explore. When this time's up, Mommy just puts her right back on the floor and starts over.

When parents pair "Uh oh" with this sort of loving action, their very young kids get a head start on learning how to behave!

Thanks for reading!

....

Potty Training
Dr. Charles Fay

What about potty training?

Some friends of mine reluctantly took my advice on this matter. Instead of reminding, lecturing, or getting frustrated, they modeled using the "potty" in front of their toddler, Anna. That's right, they used the potty in front of her and said things like, "Wow! This is great! Pretty soon you'll be old enough to use the potty too!"

Making these little "training sessions" even more powerful, they whooped, and hollered, and waved goodbye as they flushed.

Are you guessing that this caught little Anna's attention? Did she want to be "big" like her mommy and daddy? You bet!

Sure, Anna had some accidents. Instead of getting angry, her parents were empathetic, "Oh, that's sad. Well, you will learn." Then they allowed her to help by putting her diaper in the pail.

Kids potty train at different ages. All kids learn quicker when their parents aren't too embarrassed to make it fun.

Thanks for reading!

....

17

Another Strategy for Ending Bedtime Hassles
Dr. Charles Fay

One of the most common questions we're asked goes as follows:

> *What do you do when your kids won't settle down at night and start goofing around with each other? If we only had one, it'd be a lot simpler. But what do you do when all of them start acting up at once and nobody can get any sleep?*

When these sorts or problems become chronic, it's time for a Love and Logic "Strategic Training Session." Follow the steps below:

- Don't do anything until you've taken the time to plan.
- Keep all of this a secret from your kids. Consequences are often more effective when they come as a bit of a surprise to them.
- Carry out your plan only when you it's convenient for you.

Here's one mother's example:

> *Our twins kept keeping us up at night. Then we decided to put together a plan. It took two weeks to figure out how we were going to pull it off—but it was worth it. They couldn't believe it when the babysitter arrived one evening and we said, "Oh, this is so sad. We haven't been getting any sleep because you've been playing around so much at night. We're going to sleep at Aunt Dianna's house so that we can get rested up. How are you guys planning to pay your babysitter? If you don't have any money, you can pay her with some of your toys. Have a good night. We love you."*

Check out our book, *Love and Logic Magic for Early Childhood* for more ideas on solving bedtime hassles and much, much more. Thanks for reading!

Tips for Easing Separation Anxiety
Dr. Charles Fay

Nothing jerks the tears more than seeing our little sweeties melting down as we leave them with the babysitter, daycare, preschool, etc. Here's the problem: If we let our own anxiety and sadness show, our kids will pick up on it and have a much harder time adjusting to separations.

Listed below are some quick tips for easing your child's separation anxiety—and yours:

- Prior to and during separation transitions, be very business-like in your tone and general demeanor. Kids take their emotional cues from the important adults in their lives.
- Talk as little as possible. Trying too hard to reassure your child will actually elevate their fear.
- Make the transitions as quick as possible. When you leave your child, leave quickly. This is even more important if your child appears to be getting upset.
- Ask the adults you are leaving your child with how long it typically takes for them to calm down once you are gone. In most cases, it takes just a couple minutes or so.
- Enjoy your kids as much as possible when they are with you. Kids who feel secure relationships with their parents tend to experience less anxiety when they separate.

To learn more practical tips for parenting young children, watch my DVD, *Painless Parenting for the Preschool Years.*

Thanks for reading!

Don't Rush Potty Training
Dr. Charles Fay

Far too frequently, parents place undo pressure on their tots to become potty trained before they're ready. This urgency seems to come from a variety of sources, including other parents whose kids have trained earlier, preschool or daycare expectations, know-it-all relatives, and the ever-growing disgustingness (and sheer volume) of each dirty diaper.

Children are ready to master the porcelain throne at widely varying ages. I've seen some ready as early as one year of age, whereas others aren't ready until they are four or five.

How do we know when a child is ready to start learning? It's simple! They'll start pretending to use the potty, wanting to crawl up on it, wanting to flush it, and becoming generally interested in the entire process.

How do we teach them? If we want a small child to learn anything, there are three things that need to be present:

- The child needs to be physically and neurologically ready. We can't rush this!
- The child needs to see adults enthusiastically performing the skill. Yes! Our little ones need to see us using the potty with pleasure.
- The child needs to have a loving relationship with a patient and loving adult. This relationship is critical to learning. When we don't get angry about mistakes, and we don't try to punish our kids into using the potty, the process of learning becomes very natural and enjoyable.

For more information on potty training and other early childhood issues, check out our CD *Toddlers and Pre-Schoolers*.

Thanks for reading!

Toddlers and Sleeping

Dr. Charles Fay

Before I became a parent, I lacked respect for the glory of sleep. Now I know that it's wonderful to sleep, and it's even better when our little ones do it, too.

A cruel reality of parental life is that some toddlers don't need much of it. Regardless of how many times we tell them that they are tired, or lecture them about the importance of getting enough shut-eye, their inborn biorhythms don't seem to change.

Listed below are some of our opinions on the matter:

- Every toddler is different from birth.
- Some need a lot of sleep while others don't seem to.
- Trying to reason or lecture them into sleeping leaves them wider awake.
- Even if they won't sleep, they can still remain in their crib, play-pen or bedroom for some "quiet" time.
- Even if they are not quiet during "quiet" time, it's okay.
- Some kids decide to cry instead of sleeping. As long as their basic needs are being met, this is okay, too.
- The less stressed we are about making them keep their eyes and mouths closed, the happier everyone will be.
- Someday, those toddlers who don't need much sleep will become incredibly productive adults who don't need much sleep.

For more ideas about toddlers, the terrible twos, and bedtime without bedlam, see our Early Childhood Package.

Take care of yourself!

CHAPTER TWO

Seven to Twelve

Never Work Harder Than Your Kids
Dr. Charles Fay

Each afternoon, across our great nation, vast amounts of homework is completed by parents rather than their kids!

It often starts with a note from the teacher:

Dear Mrs. Mom:
Festus plays well with others and never runs with scissors, but he isn't getting his homework turned in.

Next, we find ourselves keeping a close eye on Festus to make sure he is putting pencil to paper. Of course, when he asks for help, we try to lend a hand.

Things really start to get ugly when we look up from Festus' homework assignment and discover that he has left the room!

Students of Love and Logic know about the "No sense in both of us worrying about this" syndrome. That's why they are willing to help with homework ONLY as long as their kids continue to work harder than they do.

For more tips on helping with homework, visit loveandlogic.com and see my handout titled, *Guidelines for Helping with Homework.*

Thanks for reading!

Oh, What an Energy Drain!
Dr. Charles Fay

Have you ever found yourself at a complete loss for an appropriate logical consequence? Has one of your children ever done something that's left you speechless?

Most parents answer "Yes!" to both of these questions.

Fortunately, Love and Logic offers a generic consequence—one that fits just about any thing a child might do!

The next time you find yourself stumped, have an "Energy Drain." Here are the steps:

Step #1: Say with empathy, "When you _____, it really drains my energy. We'll talk about this later.

Step #2: Give yourself some time to calm down and think.

Step #3: Ask your child how they plan to replace the energy they drained. Kid can replace energy by doing extra chores, staying home while you rest, hiring themselves a babysitter, cooking dinner, etc.

Step #4: Give them a deadline for "energy replacement," and enforce it if they forget or refuse.

Some parents find it necessary to take away a toy or do an "automatic allowance withdrawal" if their energy isn't replaced by the deadline.

Thanks for reading!

We're In This Together
Jim Fay

Are you a service/product provider instead of a parent? If so, your children are your consumers, not part of the family team. Many homes operate this way. While parents work hard to provide the best, their ungrateful children expect more and more, while making little effort to help. These children live like honored guests in the home.

This parenting style robs kids of the basic human need for being an important member of a group. It breeds hostile dependency, not loving appreciation.

Make a list of all the jobs it takes to keep your family going. Continue to add to this list and keep it on the refrigerator. This long list should include jobs like earning the money for the family, paying bills, etc. Have your children add jobs they like you to do for them. This will be an eye opener for everyone.

Once the list is finished, divide up the jobs and make everyone in the family part of the team for family survival. If you don't know how to get the kids to do their chores, listen to our audio, *"Didn't I Tell You to Take Out the Trash?"* Discover some simple rules that can change your life.

Tips for Ending Homework Hassles
Dr. Charles Fay

One mother said it well: "I'm tired of doing battle every evening over spelling words, long division, and book reports. I thought I was done with this sort of homework when I graduated from school!"

Listed below are some time-tested tips for helping your child with homework:

- **Help only as long as there is no frustration or anger.**
  When homework becomes associated with negative emotions, it's no surprise that kids start to view learning as a real drag.
- **Help only as long as your child is working harder than you are.**
  Say, "I'll be happy to help you as long as you're working harder than I am."
- **Avoid sitting with your child when they are about to "get it."**
  Many kids come to believe that they can only learn new things—or "get it"—if an adult is guiding them every step of

the way. Explain this by saying, "Part of my job as your Mom is to help you see that you can learn without me. That's why there will be times when I let you work by yourself."

Thanks for reading!

Let Them Figure It Out
Jim Fay

Some day your kids are going to need to figure things out for themselves. Wouldn't it be unfortunate if they found themselves in a dangerous or tempting situation when they get their first opportunity?

Universities report that this is often the case. Young adults are known to speed dial their parents, hand the cell phone to officials and say, "Talk to my mom. She will straighten this out."

Don't pass up an opportunity to give your kids practice figuring things out for themselves while they are still young. It's tempting in this fast-paced world to do things that kids could do for themselves. It's quicker, we're pressed for time, and it feels so good to help them.

But the bad news is that many parents pass up opportunity after opportunity to say, "I bet you can figure that out. Give it a try, I'll be here later if you need some help." Those parents put their kids at risk for believing unstated messages that say, "I have to do this because you are not capable."

To Pay, Or Not to Pay
Jim Fay

Brittney is fuming mad. Her friends get paid $20 for every A grade they get on their report card. Their B grades are worth $10.

As she tells me this she says, "My friend's parents say that grades are a kid's job, so they should be paid just like parents get paid to do their jobs. My parents keep telling me that nobody should get paid to do things that make their own lives better, and that's what getting an education is."

She goes on to complain, "And my parents are so clueless. They say that I have to do my share of the housework, and I don't get paid for that either. They're all worried that if I grow up like an honored guest in the home instead of a contributing member of the family that I'll be selfish and self-centered just like my friends! Can you believe this, they say that they don't want to addict me to anything I won't be able to earn for myself when I leave the home. I suppose they learned that out of that stupid book *From Innocence to Entitlement!*"

All I could think upon hearing this was, "Wow! How lucky she is to have great and wise parents."

....

Sometimes Our Kids Need to Tough-it-Out
Jim Fay

I had an opportunity to meet a young man who gave me great hope for the upcoming generation. When he was in sixth grade he had a teacher he didn't like. This teacher was too tough. His two best buddies agreed and they decided they needed to get out of the class.

That night they all went home with their tale of woe; Mr. Morgan was too tough, gave too much homework, tough tests, and did not tolerate tardiness.

His buddies were successful in getting out of Mr. Morgan's class; their parents didn't want them to have a teacher who might not give them "A's" and anyway, there were mornings when it was hard to get them up and to school on time.

Joe didn't do as well. His mother told him she thought Mr. Morgan's expectations were fair and what she expected of a teacher. She told Joe how lucky he was: In life, he would come across many tough—as well as some unfair—people and this experience would prepare him to deal with them successfully.

27

How did that year go for Joe? It was tough but he got all "B's" and a life lesson that has helped him become successful.

....

How Nana Nixed the Naughty Word
Jim Fay

Little kids can be clever. It's fun to make them put their brains to work. One mom told me her son had gotten into the habit of using an unacceptable phrase. All her lecturing and punishing didn't work.

Then he made the mistake of using it while Nana was babysitting. Now Nana, being your typical grandma, was always telling him how smart and wonderful he was. Because of this he tended to be extra good for her. That is, until the time he said it, "Oh, %*@#."

Nana didn't lecture or punish, she simply said, "Oh my, I don't play with boys who use that kind of language. What do you think you could say instead?"

After much thought he came up with some clever alternatives: "Oh crud." "Oh shoot." "Oh man." And Nana's favorite, "Oh criminy." Not a real word, but they liked it. They laughed as he said it over and over.

He had to put his thinking cap on to come up with it, and that's what Nana wanted. She wanted him to think before he said things that would get him in trouble.

....

The Power of the Almighty Dollar
Jim Fay

I want to thank you. Every time I think I've run out of ideas for articles, one of you will share a great success story with me. That's where these articles come from, true stories.

A dad shared this one with me: Each week his mother sends a letter and a dollar bill to his son. His son waits for those letters from Grandma with great excitement, and a little greed. The little guy loved saving those dollars. He counted and recounted them.

Money wasn't the only thing he saved. He also stored up lots of energy for when Mom and Dad went out. In fact, so much energy that he wore out every babysitter in town.

Mom finally convinced a sitter to work with her to help Junior realize the error of his ways. The deal: If he was good, Mom and Dad would pay for the sitter. If he wasn't, he paid. This got his attention.

I bet you can guess how their next night out went: A happy sitter, happy parents, and a little guy still clinging tight to those bucks.

....

What Will She Become?
Jim Fay

I bet you can predict what kind of parent this little girl will become. John Major sends this wonderful example.

Little Grace was feeling quite grown up while experiencing the wonderful feelings of being an important, contributing member of the family. She was responsible for setting the dinner table.

Coming to her daddy she asked, "Daddy, what would you like to drink with dinner? Water or milk?"

"Daddy will have a Dr. Pepper, please," was his reply.

"Oh, Daddy! That isn't one of your choices. Water or milk?"

Daddy reports that he was speechless at this point, realizing that his 4-year-old was using one of the Love and Logic techniques on him!

After about five seconds of Daddy just looking at his little girl, she said, "Daddy, if you don't choose, I'll have to choose for you."

Daddy was surprised that what came out of his mouth was, "Water!"

Isn't it great to know that Daddy's grandchildren and probably his great-grandchildren will benefit from his modeling? Refine your skills with this technique of providing choices within limits. Listen to the Love and Logic audio, *Avoiding Power Struggles With Kids*. Find it in your Love and Logic Catalog, or call us at 1-800-338-4065 to order. Thanks for reading! If you like this, get your friends on board!

Are You Doing Too Much Homework?
Dr. Charles Fay

The very best parents care deeply about how their kids do in school. That's why it's easy for them to start getting over-involved in their children's homework.

When parents sit next to their kids every night and make sure that they do each and every scrap of homework correctly, they create kids who never learn how to think and learn for themselves. Listed below are some tips for avoiding this trap:

- Provide a time and place for your child to learn and do homework.
- Help them only as long as they are doing the vast majority of the work.
- Let them know that you will let them do most of it on their own so that they won't need you to follow them to work when they are adults.
- Remember that is it far better that a child learn from getting poor grades when they are young than learn that it is someone else's responsibility to make them successful.

For a step-by-step plan for success with unmotivated kids, see our DVD titled *Hope for Underachieving Kids*.

Thanks for reading!

Wise Dad
Jim Fay

Matt was excited. One of his classmates had a new Mohawk haircut.

That evening he announced to his dad that he wanted a Mohawk. "Everybody would know who I am if I had that look. It's really cool, Dad," he exclaimed. "I'll pay for it myself. Please, Dad. Can I?"

Matt could tell, by the expression on his face, that his dad wasn't keen on the idea. However, he didn't say no. His dad believed that questions were often more powerful than statements.

"Tell me, Matt, do any of the other kids have haircuts like that?"

"Sure. He's not the only one."

"Good," replied Dad. "Go back to school and find out what the other guys are saying about those kids and their haircuts."

The next day Matt confided with his dad, "Dad, I don't think I want one of those Mohawks. The other boys think those kids are kind of weird."

When to Help With Homework
Jim Fay

Alex and Jason come home with the same math homework.

Alex complains to his mom, "It's just not fair. Mr. Jenson gives us too much homework. I don't know how to do this. He never explains anything. You need to help me. It's going to take too long!"

"How did he explain this homework?" asks mom.

"I don't remember. You need to help me," says Alex.

Mom opens the book and points out the answers. She gets the task over quickly and then lectures, "You'd better start paying attention in class!"

Jason makes the same complaint to his mom.

"How did your teacher explain this homework?" asks mom.

"I don't remember. You need to help me," says Jason.

"How sad," answers Mom. "I'll be happy to help when you work harder on your schoolwork than me, and I know that you are listening in class." With that, she tells Jason to open his book and try to remember how the teacher told him to do the work. "You can watch your program when it's finished," she tells Jason.

Which mom did the best job of parenting?

Which kid is more likely to start listening better in class?

I bet you know the answer.

Boredom

Dr. Charles Fay

Ah, the sounds of summer! Birds chirping, the sound of the ice cream truck, and kids moaning, "I'm bored! There's nothing to do."

Despite popular kid opinion, boredom is essential for the development of healthy problem-solving skills and creativity. Can you imagine the world today if Benjamin Franklin, Thomas Edison, and Henry Ford had never experienced it?

Some parents make the mistake of spending the entire summer making sure that their children are always entertained. In the process, they steal wonderful opportunities for their kids to learn creative ways to entertain themselves. They also create kids who selfishly believe that everything should be entertaining all of the time.

Wiser parents hand the boredom problem right back to their kids by responding, "That's a bummer, what do you think you are going to do?"

When their children answer, "I don't know," they simply give some suggestions and allow responsibility for solving the problem to rest on their youngsters' shoulders: "Some kids decide to draw pictures. How will that work? Other kids decide to build something out of wood. Others decide that they are going to do some reading. Good luck."

If their children continue to complain, they pat them on the back and say, "When kids keep complaining that they are bored, it means that their parents aren't giving them enough chores. There's a broom right over there."

Thanks for reading!

Transitioning to School

Dr. Charles Fay

It won't be long before our children will be expected to follow the time-honored procedures and routines of school. As parents, what can we do to up the odds that our children will easily transition from the relatively unstructured days of summer to the more demanding experience of school life?

- Avoid over-entertaining your kids during the late summer months. It's good to have plenty of fun, but your children shouldn't be so addicted to excitement that they go into shock when they have to sit quietly in a classroom.
- Maintain routines such as set family meal times and chores.
- Limit television, video games, and other highly stimulating electronic entertainment.
- Expect them to spend at least thirty minutes learning each day, by reading, writing stories, creating science projects, etc.
- Expect your older children and teens to do odd jobs around the neighborhood, get appropriate employment, or volunteer to help others in need.
- Establish the same expectations for behavior at home as they will face at school.

Thanks for reading!

....

My Bully Child
Dr. Charles Fay

At Love and Logic we've spent a good deal of time and energy talking about what parents can do if their children are being picked on at school. Sally Ogden's book, *Words Will Never Hurt Me* is a wonderful resource for helping kids who are being victimized.

But what do we do if our child is the one doing the bullying?

- With great empathy, inform your child that it really drains your energy when you find out that they've been hassling other kids.
- Expect them to replace the energy they've drained by doing extra chores, hiring someone to watch them, etc.
- Expect them to do something nice for the victim, as well as the

teachers who've had to deal with the problem at school. Saying, "I'm sorry" is not enough.

- Kids with a second or third grade reading ability may benefit from doing a book report on *Words Will Never Hurt Me*.
- Address the underlying hurt within your child by providing even more love and attention. Don't hesitate to get professional help if the problem continues.

Thanks for reading!

Don't Pay Kids To Be Good
Jim Fay

"Can you believe it?" seven-year-old Kayla's mom moaned to her friend. "I have to take her with me to my cleaning job. She drives me nuts getting into everything she's not supposed to touch. I have to pay her to be good or she drives me crazy. It worked for a while, but now that's not even working. Yesterday she told me that I wasn't paying her enough!"

Mom's mistake of paying or bribing her child to be good ranks close to the top of mistakes parents make. If she keeps this up she will soon suffer from "extortion inflation." By the time Kayla becomes a teen, no amount of money will buy good behavior.

How many times have you heard parents in the store saying, "Now if you're good, I'll let you buy a treat"? Every time I hear this I have fantasies of shaking the parent, or at least yelling, "BIG MISTAKE!"

Recently I watched two young boys following their dad into the store as they were saying, "Daddy, what do we get if we're good in the store today?"

His answer was, "A happy family. That's what you get!"

Now there's a dad I like!

By the way, Kayla's mom needs to listen to our CD, *Love and Logic Magic When Kids Drain Your Energy*. The technique specified there would work on Kayla.

All The Other Kids Get to Do It!

Dr. Charles Fay

If your kids are old enough to talk, you've probably heard things like:

- "Carmen's parents let her watch anything on TV she wants to."
- "Mandy gets to have her computer in her room. Like, this is the 21st century."

Some of us have even heard horrifying things like:

- "Ray's parents buy him beer for his parties. What's the big deal?" or,
- "Julie's mom doesn't care if her boyfriend spends the night in her room. Her mom trusts her."

My message for this week is a simple one:

Our kids learn to resist peer pressure by seeing us do it.

If we back down when our kids argue, manipulate, and try to use guilt, they're far more likely to do the same when their friends turn up the heat. In the CD, *Hormones and Wheels,* Jim and Foster teach a variety of techniques for staying strong through the pre-teen and teen years. One of the handiest involves responding to arguments by calmly repeating the same loving one-liner, such as "I love you too much to argue," "Probably so," or "What did I say?"

"I argue at 6 a.m. on Saturdays" is my personal favorite for the teen years.

Doing this will make them mad in the short term, while teaching them how to live happier, healthier lives in the long term.

Teen Credit Cards — Do Leave Home Without It?
Jim Fay and Kristan Leatherman

Dad: (teasingly) "Have you made your list for Santa?"

Brianna: "Santa's for kids, Dad. I'm 10 years old. I don't need to make a list this year. I just want one thing."

Dad: "One thing?!"

Brianna: "Yep!"

Dad: "Well that's really admirable! Especially in these materialist and gluttonous times. What's the one thing?"

Brianna: "A credit card!"

Brianna, like many of her peers, understands enough about Dad's shiny little plastic card to know that it can buy her anything she wants. But in this case, it's what she doesn't know that is even more important.

Dad would be wise to give Brianna lots and lots of practice borrowing and paying back loans on time in full. Kids who get those kinds of learning experiences will eventually become credit card–wise if we allow them the chance to both succeed and fail with money tools that don't carry the risk of "buy now, pay later."

Love and Logic teaches that it's not a good idea to teach kids how to spend money they don't have. Wise parents do not co-sign for credit cards, or allow their children to use their credit cards, until they reach the legal age to have their own. Introduce your kids to cash first, followed by prepaid and debit cards, as training wheels for a credit card.

We hope your college age sons or daughters are armed with a solid understanding of what credit means before they receive their first credit card solicitation.

Bottom line: It's not the credit card, but fiscal responsibility that our children shouldn't leave home without!

Learn more about preparing kids to become credit card savvy in our book, *Millionaire Babies or Bankrupt Brats?*

Thanks for reading!

36

Thinking for Himself
Jim Fay

After reading *Parenting With Love and Logic*, Tim's mom instituted a new bedtime policy. She told Tim that picking a sleep time was his decision. He was expected to be in his room at 8:00 each evening, but he could decide when to go to sleep. In addition to this, everyone in the family was to have "feet on the floor" at 6:00 a.m. No exceptions.

Tim slept through his alarm the next morning, only to discover that the family was leaving the house without him. A rather unpleasant babysitter took over and charged him for her services.

Needless to say, he was ready the next morning. This continued through the last four weeks of school. All during summer vacation, much to his liking, he got to sleep longer.

Now that school was soon to open, Tim came to his mom with an idea. "Mom, I'm going to run some experiments. I'm going to set my alarm for 6:00 a.m. Will you get me out of bed no matter how much I complain?"

"Now why would you want me to do that, Tim?"

"I'm running some experiments. Each night I'm going to go to bed a little later until I figure out how late I can go to sleep and still wake up in time. Since it's my decision, I better learn how to make it a good one."

You'll enjoy the story about bedtime at the Fay's in my CD "Helicopters, Drill Sergeants, and Consultants."

Thanks for reading.

Donovan's Gloves
Jim Fay

Dave Funk, one of our very favorite Love and Logic experts, has two adopted kids, Donovan and Ski. He writes about Donovan's experience with responsibility:

Like many 12-year-old boys, wearing gloves in even a cold Wisconsin winter was not "cool." In his attempt to avoid even the temptation to do so, he "lost" them—they were nowhere to be found. In the winter, about his only source of income is snow removal. This particular year in Wisconsin it was cold and record snow. On one occasion Donovan was to shovel and I "noticed" he didn't have any gloves. He said he didn't need any; however, the temperature was below 20 degrees and the steel handle on the snow blower was the same. After about five minutes, Donovan asked if he could use my gloves. I acknowledged the fact that cold hands are miserable and that although I would not lend my gloves, I would rent them for fifty cents. When I paid Donovan for his work, the envelope had a bit of math on it: $10.00 for the work he did on the driveway minus fifty cents for the glove rental. That was on a Sunday. Interestingly enough, the next day Donovan "found" his gloves. One was in his school locker, the other was under his bed. He had this same pair at the ready for the rest of the season.

Dave tells many stories in his book, *Getting Special Kids Ready for the Real World*. These examples apply to all kids. It is a great read with powerful techniques.

Make the Time Fit the Crime
Jim Fay

Eleven-year-old Quigley was incensed. "My teacher's never fair. Just because the bus driver got mad at us on the field trip, she's not letting me go out to recess for a whole week!"

"Well, you shouldn't have been acting up on the bus. I told you not to sit with Jake. You know what happens when the two of you get together. He's a bad influence on you."

"Yeah, but recess doesn't have anything to do with the bus! I could understand if I was bad on recess, not getting to go to recess. She doesn't like me. You need to go to school and tell her it's not fair!"

Quigley has some wisdom here. Kids are more likely to learn from consequences when they can make a reasonable connection between their behavior and the punishment. Consequences need to match the time and place of the misbehavior.

Fortunately, Mom knows that Quigley's having to live with the unfair punishment is far less damaging than her pleading his case with the teacher.

"Yes, Quigley. It probably isn't fair. Would you like to hear what some other kids have tried at times like this?" She then used the Love and Logic technique, "Guiding Kids to Own and Solve Their Own Problems."

Mom knew that his dealing with his own problem with her advice would make him stronger. Her solving it for him would make him weaker and more dependent.

You can learn about this technique on our audio CD, *Four Steps to Responsibility*, just one of the 6 CDs in *The Life Saver Kit*. *The Life Saver Kit* is a complete collection of great parenting techniques.

Thanks for reading!

....

Make Them Part of the Family
Jim Fay

I last wrote about the importance of kids contributing to the work-load of the family. One of our basic human needs is to be needed and to be a part of a family. When children live their lives as guests in a four star hotel instead of as a contributing member of a family, this basic need is denied. The usual result is for them to feel increasingly resentful without knowing why.

One way to help a child feel needed, important, and valued in the family is to put him/her in charge of one family meal per week. This means planning, cooking, serving, and cleaning up. Most kids are capable of doing this by the time they are eight years old.

Of course the quality of the food will suffer temporarily while they are in training mode. But this changes dramatically as they learn and become excited about being able to cook.

Many parents report to us that their kids resist at first, but soon think that they enjoy cooking. In many cases, what the kids enjoy and don't recognize are the wonderful feelings of being valued.

Thanks for reading!

P.S. You can learn more about involving kids in the family workload in Pearl #7 in the book, *Parenting With Love and Logic.* Another good resource is the audio CD, *"Didn't I Tell You To Take Out The Trash?"*

CHAPTER THREE

Teens

Breaking Promises

Jim Fay

Sixteen year-old Josh was livid, "Mom, you promised! You said that I'd get a car when I was sixteen. You always expect me to keep my promises!"

Mom was frustrated and confused. She'd made that promise two years ago. Part of her believed that she was obligated to live with her promise. The other part of her realized that Josh was now drinking with his friends. She was terrified that this could lead to a driving tragedy. What should she do?

The answer is that promises can only be made with the assumption that conditions will remain the same. However, there are times when conditions change and the basis for the promise is no longer valid.

Mom needs to answer Josh with, "This is sad. I decided to make that promise based on not worrying about alcohol use. I could have kept the promise if things had stayed the same. Now that I worry about your use of alcohol I have a responsibility to change my decision."

It is often helpful to explain this to children at the time a promise is made.

Getting the Most for the Money
Jim Fay

Britney and Tami's parents decided that their young teens could benefit from having their own clothing allowance. Today was the first time that the girls could do their very own shopping.

Britney took her mother to the mall and made her purchases. When it was Tami's turn she went to one of the bargain stores.

That evening the girls were to have a fashion show for Dad, modeling all their new outfits.

Out came Britney. She was wearing a very fashionable outfit with matching accessories.

She then sat with Dad while Tami made her appearance. To Britney's chagrin, Tami came out again and again, each time with a different outfit on.

As Britney waited for her next clothing allowance, due in four months, she tired of her one outfit. Mom and Dad expressed their empathy and said, "Not to worry, Sweetie. You'll have another opportunity soon. It'll be interesting to see how you handle your money."

"Did You Do Drugs?"
Jim Fay

"Hey, Dad. Did you and Mom do drugs when you were young?"

Look out, parents! This is not a simple childhood question. This is a kid looking for some leverage and a way to get some tacit approval for drug use. This is a kid looking for the opportunity to say, "Well you did it too."

If you didn't use drugs it is a great chance to explain why you didn't. If you did, you might want to consider this reply. "Yes, I was very foolish and tried some drugs. But I was lucky to have people who showed me what they were doing to me. I saw my friends having horrible problems. Their grades went down. Their family lives were in shambles, and two of them died of overdoses. Then one day I realized that I wanted a family some day, and I thought how humiliated I would be to have to honestly talk about how foolish I was. So that's why I quit and why I hope you never have to be as humiliated as I am when your own kids ask this question."

Is Your Teen Really Ready to be Safe Behind the Wheel?
Dr. Charles Fay

Decrease the odds of tragedy by asking yourself the following questions:

- **Does my teen respectfully follow the rules of the home and school?** If a teen is unable to follow simple rules about respect, chores, etc., they aren't ready for the complex rules of the road.
- **Does my teen know how to cope with frustration in a calm way?** If a teen is prone to fits of anger, the chances of road rage are high.
- **Is my teen willing to limit the number of passengers in the car?** The more passengers, the greater the likelihood of tragedy.
- **Does my teen have a safe driving record so far?** The best predictor of future behavior is past behavior.
- **Is my teen making a significant financial—or "sweat"—investment in the driving?** The more a teen invests in his or her car, its maintenance, and insurance, the safer they will drive.

If the answer to any of these questions is "No," it's time to share this tip with your teen and say:

You may drive again when I am sure that I can answer "Yes" to all of these questions.

Thanks for reading!

"Why Won't You Let Me?"
Jim Fay

It might be comforting to know that you don't have to be able to provide a good reason for saying no to your kids. Our kids are not our supervisors. If something doesn't feel right to you, that's a good enough reason to say no. The best parents have the courage to say no when their intuition warns them about a situation even if they cannot put the reason into words.

Fifteen-year-old Will used to be successful getting his way. Every time his dad said no, he demanded an explanation for Dad's refusal. Dad would give in whenever he could not put his reason into words. All this came to a screeching halt the day Dad learned to say, "If you don't figure this out by the time you have kids your age, come and see me."

Will would try to argue, but Dad only repeated, "So, what did I say?" Arguing no longer paid off for Will.

Choices, Choices, Choices
Jim Fay

Love and Logic parents know the power in giving choices to children. The more choices we give, the more control we get back. The wise parent is constantly looking for opportunities to give choices about issues that make no difference to them. Then when important decisions need to be made, or decisions that affect others they can say, "Wait a minute. You've had your turn to decide. Now it's mine. Thanks for understanding."

Fifteen year-old Travis was riding in the car with Mom and her friend. He announced that the music they were listening to was stupid and changed the station to the one he liked. Mom's friend was shocked to hear his mother say, "I study Love and Logic and it teaches that kids need to make choices."

Is Travis' mother right? Of course not! She has created a spoiled brat by allowing him to make choices that affect others. Travis needs some limits in his life.

....

Why Won't He Get a Job?
Jim Fay

Jerry's mom is frustrated. "I'm on my last nerve with that kid. I've told him that he needs to get a job this summer. All he wants to do is lay around the house. It would be different if he was willing to help out around here, but he doesn't do a thing!"

I was the fifth person at the party to be approached with her complaints. I guess she was getting a lot of sympathy from everybody who listened to her sad story.

"Where is he getting money to continue this lifestyle?" I asked.

With slumping shoulders she answered, "From me. Where else?"

Bingo! Now we see the problem. It's not the lazy kid. It's the sucker who provides the money, thus eliminating the need for a job.

Love and Logic teaches that there are three possible solutions to a problem:

- Remove the child from the situation if that is appropriate.
- Remove the adult from the situation if that is appropriate.
- Remove the offending object.

In this case Mom needs to remove the money. It's the offending object.

People usually look for work when the free handouts are removed.

When Jerry asks why she is no longer giving money, she can answer, "Sorry, it became a problem."

....

The Paper Route Saga
Jim Fay

Timmy lived in a family where money was tight. He wished he could buy some of the things his friends had. His solution was to get a paper route with 120 customers.

It was fun at first, but having to get up at 4:30 a.m. every morning became a chore. It was too much like work. So, before long he was sleeping through his alarm.

Mom worried about the customers. She worried about his him losing his job. She nagged Timmy without results. Then she turned on her husband. "You are going to have to set your alarm each morning so you can help Timmy. It's just too hard for him and I don't want him to lose his job."

Dad refused, saying, "It's not my job." Mom started getting up each morning at 4:30.

Finally mom Mom figured it out. "Wait a minute. What would be worse? Would it be worse for him to lose his dream job some day for lack of responsibility, or would it be better for him to learn that lesson on a low low-paying job at age 15?"

She knew the answer. She called his supervisor and warned him that she didn't contract for the job and that Timmy was on his own. Wise mom!

Are You a "Cool" Parent?
Jim Fay

Have your kids tried this argument yet?

"But other parents, like, let their kids have beer at their parties. You guys are like so last century. All the other parents are always there to make sure no one gets like really drunk. Why can't you be cool like all the other parents?"

Our job as parents is not to be cool. Our job is not to be their friends or to be product and service providers for our kids. Our job is to model good behavior. We teach character, responsibility, honesty, etc., by our example.

So, how do you handle this situation? When they say, "But other parents do it," you respond with, "In this house we don't ask each other to break the law. Thank you."

When you let underage kids drink, you send the message that they can choose which laws they want to obey. It doesn't take long for them to decide that they can choose which of your rules to obey.

Do your kids a favor. Teach them responsible behavior, and don't give in. It will pay off in the long run, and in some cases, even save their lives.

A Stranger in Your Home
Dr. Charles Fay

The door bell rings, and there he stands. He's about forty, of average height and weight, and he's a complete stranger. Before you have a chance to speak, he says, "I was in the neighborhood, and I just thought I'd stop by and spend some unsupervised time with your twelve-year-old in her room."

What's the likelihood that you'd let him in?

While you'd never consider allowing a stranger into your child's room, there's an epidemic of parents who are doing just that by allowing their kids to have computers in their rooms so that they can have private chat sessions with their "friends."

There is absolutely no reason for a child to have a computer in their room, particularly one connected to the Internet. Responsible parents put the computer where it and their children are easily supervised. They explain this by saying, "Believe it or not, there are plenty of really smart and responsible kids like you who are getting tricked by really bad people through the Internet."

If their kids try to argue, they repeat with empathy, "I love you too much to argue about this."

Thanks for reading!

The Trust Card
Jim Fay

Teenagers often pull out the trust card defense. It sounds like, "Don't you trust me?" or "You don't trust me." Believe me. When they say this they have something to hide. So the best parental response is, "You're right. That's my job. You can trust that I will do everything I can to help you see when you are putting yourself in harm's way."

Wise parents know that teens often fail to see the dangers in their actions due to lack of experience. They thrive on a system of insider information to trick parents. Peers, advertising, and predators easily mislead kids this age. So it is our job to know what they are doing and be available for advice or placing limits.

Here are some words you can use sometime.

> *"I know that you are a good kid. Where things can go wrong for you is when you make decisions based on your smarts without the wisdom that comes from experience. My job is to share experience that only comes from seeing things go wrong. I can only do that when I know what you are facing. So don't take it personally if I seem to be nosey or if I don't trust everything you tell me. I love you too much to neglect my job."*

You'll find more like this in our updated book, *Parenting Teens With Love and Logic.*

A Sobering Thought
Jim Fay

A recent national poll conducted by Ameriquest Mortgage Company found that today's kids spend 500 percent more than their parents did at the same age, adjusted for inflation.

Ask yourself where your kids spent this money. Was it on basic necessities, conveniences, or status? Then ask yourself what percentage of the money spent on conveniences and status was actually earned by your children. Now ask yourself how much of the convenience and status they have is a result of your not being able to say no to their pleading, demanding, and extortion.

Many of today's children have no idea how much work and self-discipline it takes to get these things.

As we move into a global economy, your kids are going to have to compete for jobs with kids in other countries who are hungry right now. These are kids who believe that the path to success is self-discipline and hard work, not entitlement.

If your kids are not earning the grades they get, working for the things they want, doing their fair share of the work, and treating family members with respect, their economic future is at risk.

It's possible that a child from an underdeveloped nation who is starving for your kid's future job may very well be the one who wins it.

Study: Love and Logic's *Setting Limits* audio CD to learn how to say no when faced with begging, demanding, or extortion.

Thinking About Growing Up

Jim Fay

Fifteen-year-old Jason was feeling independent. He and his friends all agreed that their parents were "clueless" and had no right to be asking them to be slaves around the house this summer. They had already had a stressful time just making it through another year of school. That was enough. Now was the time to chill out and hang out.

The only problem was that Jason's friends had parents who were providing plenty of ready cash. In Jason's eyes, his parents should do the same, but they had taken a Love and Logic course and were expecting him to do his share of the work around the house and were outrageous enough to suggest that he earn some of his own spending money.

Being turned down for a "loan" to buy the latest gadget, Jason sarcastically retorted, "Yeah, I know. It's time I started to grow up get a job and earn what I want!" With this he stomped off.

Dad was so proud of himself. He didn't even respond. But later, when all had settled down, he did bring it up. "Jason, a while ago you mentioned that it might be time for you to grow up, get a job, and start earning what you want. I've thought about it and think that you might really be on to something there."

Needless to say, Jason stomped off again. But he left with plenty to think about.

Hone your skills with teenagers. Listen to *Hormones and Wheels* each day on your way home from work.

Upping the Odds That Your Teen Will Be a Safe Driver
Dr. Charles Fay

I worry terribly about teens with parents who buy them cars and pay for all of the other costs of driving. These kids are far more likely to make tragic life-ending errors of judgment than those who have to really work for the privilege. Why's this so? Simply because teenagers don't fear death; but they do fear financial loss.

As soon as possible—even as early as the elementary grades—start the following conversation with your kids:

Parent: "I sure hope that you can afford to drive some day."
Child: "What? Everybody drives."
Parent: "Only those people who have the money. How are you planning to save so that you can afford to pay for most of it when you're 16?"
Child: "Uh?"
Parent: "I want you to be able to drive. A lot of kids decide to start a savings account and save money from their birthdays, Christmas, odd jobs, etc."

Really responsible kids are far more likely to become really responsible drivers! That's why we've teamed up with Public Television stations across the country to produce a show titled, "How to

Raise Kids Who Make Responsible Decisions." We believe that this show can save many lives. Please help us with this goal by contacting your local Public Television station and requesting that they air the program.

It's not too late if your child is already driving! In my mind, it's far better to have a teen who's temporarily angry than one who's permanently gone.

Thanks for reading!

Peer Pressure
Jim Fay

> "*The more a child's life is micro-managed, the more susceptible* he/she becomes to peer pressure."

Some parents actually train their kids to listen to peer pressure. The process is simply a matter of teaching kids to listen to a voice outside their own heads during the early years when their brains are still operating in a very concrete way.

Granted, there are times when we must take charge and tell kids exactly what to do and when to do it. However, when this becomes a pattern it gradually convinces children that the most important voice is the one that comes from others.

Many parents lock in this belief by responding to bad decisions with, "See. You should have listened to me."

Once their brain starts to develop abstract thinking, kids say, "I'm growing up. I can think for myself." Sadly, their brain has been trained to listen to the outside voice, and I bet you've already guessed where that voice is going to come from: their peers.

So when you hear a parent say that their kid has changed now that he is a teen, you can think, "Maybe not. He just listens to a different voice now."

Foster and I discuss ways to avoid this on page 229 of *Parenting Teens With Love and Logic.*

51

Opportunities
Jim Fay

Self-confidence, responsibility, character, and resiliency all find their foundation in the same place. They grow out of the opportunities children create when they make poor decisions and are faced with the consequences that follow.

Wise parents over-ride their own natural tendencies to rescue or to tell kids how to deal with these opportunities. If they don't, the opportunities are lost. Over a period of time, youngsters start to believe that others are smarter and more capable than they are.

Jake called his dad from college to say that his car had been towed. He tried to explain that it wasn't his fault because the parking sign was not easy to see.

Dad replied, "Oh, that is sad. What do you think you are going to do?"

"Well, Dad, I was thinking you need to send me $200 so I can get the car out of the impound lot."

"Yes, son. That would be nice, but since I didn't park the car, I'm not paying to get it back. Let me know how you work it out."

Jake called back later to talk to Mom, saying that he had applied for three different jobs.

"I don't want to talk to Dad right now. I want to wait until I have the job and solve this problem. Then he'll be really proud of me."

Now that's what I call a classic opportunity. Dad handed the problem back and the son discovered how capable he was.

By the way, I'm out on the road a lot. If you recognize me in the airport or at my conferences, don't be a stranger! Come up and introduce yourself.

Turning Star Bucks into Big Bucks
Jim Fay

Insider tip excerpt from *Millionaire Babies or Bankrupt Brats?*

Darren, 16 years old, begins his school day as often as he can with his favorite drink — triple mocha espresso, extra foam, extra hot. Not a big deal, from Darren's perspective, but a VERY BIG DEAL from a financial perspective.

Here's the real jolt.

Let's say he buys a cup of coffee before going to work each morning for a year (50 weeks x 5 days = 250 days). After each preference is added in, and a tip, let's say it costs $4.

Now if he saved that money instead, by the end of the first year he would be $1,000 richer. And if he invested that $1,000 each year at 9% until he was 61, he'd be $574,186.02 richer.

Otherwise, he's investing in a one half million dollar mocha!

Perhaps Darren should consider saving his money instead — and make his own coffee.

If he did, when Darren is 61 years old, he'll probably be a little less jittery on two counts!

Bottom Line: Wise parents use everyday spending examples to teach their children the power of choice and the wisdom of investing early and often.

....

Help Your Kids Spot the Cycle of Abuse
Dr. Charles Fay

I was repulsed and dismayed—yet not surprised. The television images flashed before my eyes. It wasn't the first time I'd seen video of teenage girls bashing the daylights out of a helpless peer. You probably saw the same images of the Florida teens who committed this horrific act. If you're like me, it leaves you thinking, "How can I prevent this from happening to my kid?"

The sobering fact is that we can do everything right with our kids and bad things can still happen to them. Nevertheless, there are a few things we can teach our kids that will decrease the odds that they'll find themselves in this sort of situation:

One involves helping them understand the cycle of abuse. Typically, this cycle starts with the perpetrator doling out relatively small types of maltreatment, such as ignoring the victim or using biting sarcasm.

During the next step in the cycle, perpetrators will often act like they are sorry, or will do something sweet that leaves the victims thinking that they will be treated better in the future.

Just as the victims becomes more at ease, the perpetrators dish out a higher level of abuse, such as name calling, starting horrible rumors, etc.

Next the perpetrators will act like they are sorry, lulling the victims into thinking that all is okay.

When the victims let down their guard, the perpetrators execute an even greater level of violence. Each time the cycle spins, the violence becomes more severe, eventually resulting in severe physical and emotional abuse…sometimes death.

It's helpful for our kids to understand this cycle. Why? So that they can spot when it's happening…and protect themselves before the violence escalates.

Thanks for reading!

....

Angry Youth
Dr. Charles Fay

Working in a treatment center for emotionally disturbed, often violent, teens I learned just a thing or two. First, never wear a tie to work. Second, the people who enjoy the best success with these youngsters understand how they think and perceive the world.

Research has revealed that aggressive kids:

- Tend to misperceive others' intentions and behaviors as personally threatening.
- Have elevated levels of physiological arousal, leaving them always on the verge of blowing their tops.
- Believe that being embarrassed by someone is justification for revenge.
- In an attempt to maintain their negative view of the world, often trick adults into behaving almost as aggressively as they do.

In my CD, *Angry and Oppositional Students*, I teach five principles for success:

1. Send positive relationship messages. These kids have to know that we care and are not going to give up on them.
2. Use nonthreatening, calm body language.
3. Provide friendly supervision in unstructured settings. Glaring at kids in the hall just creates sneakier kids.
4. Never embarrass or single them out in front of the group.
5. Provide discipline only when it's safe. Wise adults delay consequences and meet with the child when they are calm and other adults are nearby.

Thanks for reading!

Phone Tossing
Jim Fay

Dad bought Cindy a new cell phone and before long he had two frustrations.

It became more and more difficult to talk with her because of her distraction with text messaging her friends. When she wasn't talking or texting she was absentmindedly tossing the phone in the air and catching it.

Being very athletic, she seldom missed the catch, but when she did, the phone crashed to the floor. Dad was becoming more and more concerned that the phone would break and she would be begging for a replacement.

Warning her about damage to the phone was like talking to the wall. When she did respond, it was with, "Oh, Dad. Give it a rest. You worry too much."

Over the weekend Dad listened to the audio CD, *Love Me Enough to Set Some Limits.* Since threatening and reminding didn't work, he couldn't wait to try out a new approach.

Armed with new skills, he caught Cindy in mid-throw with, "Hey Cindy. I thought I ought to let you know that I don't buy replacement phones for those that are tossed around."

This didn't stop the tossing right away, but Dad noticed that the throws gradually became shorter and less frequent. Then they stopped altogether.

Cindy had to let her father know that, "I stop when I say stop, not when you say stop!"

Wise parents know that giving information and then waiting works better than demanding an immediate response.

Lear more about setting limits on the CD, *Love Me Enough to Set Some Limits.*

....

Actions Beat Threats
Jim Fay

Dad, talking to Sara last evening in the Jackson home:

"Wow! Look at this cell phone bill. You went $180.00 over your text messaging allotment. What is the matter with you young lady? I don't see how you can throw away money like that. We're going to have some rules around here. You're going to have to learn a little responsibility. How do you expect me to keep paying for this kind of nonsense? If this happens again you are in big trouble!"

Dad, talking to his friend this morning at work:

"Sara went over her text messaging allotment again this month. I had to really lay down the law to her last night. I don't know why kids have to spend so much money on those phones and then just blow it off like it's no big deal."

Dad's friend: "This is out of control. What are you going to do?"

Dad: "If this keeps up, I'm going to have to take her phone away."

Jim Fay, thinking to himself:

Dad is all talk and no action. He is a little late taking action. He should have taken the phone the first time she abused the privilege. When she asked why, he should have said, "The phone has become a problem. Some day when you've paid me back for this I'll consider returning it."

Sure, she will argue and complain and make threats of her own. That's why Love and Logic parents use, "I love you too much to argue," to neutralize the arguing.

Taking action trumps complaining and threatening every time.

This dad needs to listen to "Hormones and Wheels" on the way home from work each day.

Thanks for reading!

Sweet Aunt Sara
Jim Fay

Do you make your kids do chores? Some parents think their kids have too much going on with school, extra-curricular activities, jobs, etc., to help around the house. This can have negative consequences. Jim Fay explains:

Sweet Aunt Sara has reached an advanced age. She is now so feeble that she can't take care of herself. You bring her into your home with the intention of making her remaining years comfortable. Since she is not strong enough to help out around the house, and knows that, you tell her that she no longer needs to help. You will take care of her every need.

Wouldn't you think that she'd be so appreciative that she'd become sweeter and sweeter by the day? Not so. You and I both know this is not what happens. In turn, she becomes increasingly difficult to live with. Why is this?

This phenomenon is known as hostile dependency. Embedded in the human soul is the drive to be independent. It is common to hate the feeling of dependency and quickly transfer the blame to those who make us feel dependent. Their good intentions are soon forgotten, as anger sets in.

This situation is often seen in teenagers who live like honored guests in the home; those whose parents don't expect them to do their fair share of the work around the house; those parents who treat their kids just as we are treating sweet Aunt Sara.

Do your kids and yourself a favor. Expect every member of the family to share in the workload.

Next week I'll give you some valuable tips about how to do this.

In the meantime listen to the CD, *"Didn't I Tell You To Take Out The Trash?"* for ideas about how to turn this around.

Thanks for reading!

Curfews: To Set Them or Not
Dr. Charles Fay

Curfews are an inevitable part of parenting. They can be sources of conflict or you can use them as learning experiences. Dr. Charles Fay explains:

Those of you familiar with Love and Logic have probably already noticed that we are rather old-fashioned codgers. We believe that parents should run the home rather than the kids.

Now for the shocker: In our book, "Parenting Teens with Love and Logic", we teach that parents are typically better off if they allow their teens to negotiate a reasonable time to be home each evening. "Reasonable" is the key here. Depending on the kid, the activity they are involved in, the degree of responsible adult supervision, the weather, the type of community we live in, etc., a "reasonable" time to be home might range from 6 PM to the wee hours of the morning.

The key is showing that we are more concerned about their emotional, physical, and spiritual safety than whether we can make them come home at a certain time. Expressing worry about their safety results in far less rebellion than trying to dictate an arbitrary time for them to walk back over the threshold.

"We need the phone numbers of the people you will be with so that we can find you if something goes wrong," is also a wise and reasonable request to make. Doing a little detective work to keep them honest never hurts, either!

Here's the overall goal: Get your teens setting their own reasonable curfews so that they will be good at it by the time they turn eighteen and leave home.

Thanks for reading!

CHAPTER FOUR

All Ages

Importance of Empathy
Dr. Charles Fay

What's the very most important Love and Logic skill?

EMPATHY!

Understanding why is fairly simple. Consequences delivered with empathy create responsibility. Consequences delivered without empathy create resentment.

So we have a choice: Will we raise responsible kids or resentful ones?

Will we end up in a nice nursing home or a nasty one?

Yes. Understanding why empathy is the most important skill is simple. Empathy preserves the relationship and makes it very hard for our kids to blame us for their poor decisions.

Really using sincere empathy on a consistent basis is the hard part!

We've spend over two decades studying people who've been successful with this. What do they have in common? They use just one empathetic statement—regardless of what consequence they must provide.

That's right. They keep it simple!

61

They also pick one that fits their personality and culture. Some folks always precede consequences with, "That is so sad." Others prefer, "Oh, man … "

Some parents say, "What a bummer." Others prefer, "Bless your heart."

Tape this note on your bathroom mirror as a reminder.

Thanks for reading!

Don't Give Your Kids the Message of Entitlement
Jim Fay

I met a family who appeared to have great teenagers. "Yes, they are," offered Mom. "I worked hard with them when they were little, and it really paid off. They were expected to behave and help out with the family jobs. Now they are a joy."

Unfortunately the third child in the family was nothing like the older ones. With remorse Mom told us that by the time he came along she was worn out. "I no longer had the energy, so my way was to just give him what he wanted. I didn't want the hassle."

She went on to say that this was the worst mistake of her life. "He's not like the other kids. He's lazy and selfish. All he wants to do is watch TV and play video games. He's never happy unless he gets his way."

Mom has discovered how to create an entitled child who will probably never be happy. Now she has to decide to continue the damage to her child or to start setting some limits.

The good news is that it's not too late if she learns to use Love and Logic.

When Consequences Don't Work
Dr. Charles Fay

When Jason turned fifteen, his mother heard about Love and Logic. With every spare moment, she read our books, listened to our CDs, and attended our seminars.

He kept misbehaving. In desperation, she asked, "Why won't he learn from the consequences I provide?" Listed below are some thoughts I asked her to ponder:

Thought #1: **Am I expecting him to thank me for using Love and Logic?**
Things tend to look worse in the short term.

Thought #2: **Am I remembering the sincere empathy?**
Nothing works without it.

Thought #3: **Am I using too many words?**
A reminder, warning, or lecture will make any consequence ineffective.

Thought #4: **Am I focusing too heavily on the negative?**
Notice at least ten positive things for every negative.

Thought #5: **Does this child need professional help?**
If you're concerned that Love and Logic is not working, it's never a bad idea to get a professional opinion.

Thanks for reading!

Are Your Kids Making Enough Mistakes?
Dr. Charles Fay

Have you noticed that it's pretty easy to "slip" out of the Love and Logic habit? If you're like most of us, you've already noticed how easy it is to start forgetting the "new" and sliding right back into the "old."

A major part of the "old" for most folks is the belief that "good" parents and teachers make sure that kids don't misbehave or make mistakes.

Fans of Love and Logic know that mistakes are actually golden opportunities for kids to become prepared for the real world. They also remember that mistakes suffer from inflation—as youngsters grow bigger, so do the consequences of their actions.

Our hope for all children is that they will make plenty of small mistakes when they are young so they don't have to make extremely costly, possibly deadly, ones when they are older.

Might it be wise to post the following note on your bathroom mirror?

Are my kids making enough little mistakes?

Thanks for reading!

Getting a Little Help
Jim Fay

Blaine was upset. "You'd think I could get a little help from the family, but oh, no. Every time I need my kids or husband to help it's like pulling teeth. What's the matter with them? Why can't they help without copping an attitude?"

It didn't take long to identify the problem. Each time Blaine wanted someone to help, her request started with a criticism. Instead of saying, "I need some help in the kitchen", she complained, "Why don't you ever help me in the kitchen?" When she wanted the kids to take out the trash, she said, "Can't you see that the trash is piling up?"

64

Blaine would probably get a lot more cooperation if she could learn to focus on letting others know what would make her happy instead of dwelling on what makes her unhappy.

"I could really use some help, thanks."

"I'd appreciate your taking out the trash, thank you."

Most people lose their desire to help when confronted with criticism, but feel good about being able to help when they are not criticized.

Tough Teachers: Why Your Kids Need at Least One
Dr. Charles Fay

While the vast majority of educators deserve great praise for their patience, care, and competence, most of us have known at least one who scowled instead of smiled, yelled instead of whispered, and pointed out our weaknesses instead of our strengths.

As parents, it's tempting to rescue our kids from such teachers— to demand that our kids be moved to another class.

My parents felt this temptation when I was in the third grade.

I still regard Mrs._____(name deleted to protect the guilty) as one of the most negative, demanding, and cold people I've ever met.

She did me a great favor!

After the first week of school, my mom and dad patted me on the back and said, "You are so lucky. This year you're going to learn how to do something that plenty of adults haven't learned yet! This year you're going to learn all about how to get along with really tough people. We will help you with ideas."

I wasn't impressed! But they were right!

When your kids meet Mrs. _____, will you give them this gift or steal it from them?

Thanks for reading!

Defiance
Jim Fay

Jason was a defiant kid. His standard response was, "No, you can't make me!"

His mother developed a Love and Logic Strategic Training Session.

After plugging the holes in the plan with the help of her friends, she set up an exciting activity for Saturday. During dinner on Friday evening Jason became belligerent about something. Mom asked him to go to his room for some recovery time.

"I don't have to. You can't make me!" screamed Jason.

"Did I ask in a nice way, Jason?" asked his mom.

"I'm still not going," he shouted.

Mom dropped it and allowed him to think that he got away with being defiant.

When it was time to leave the house on Saturday morning, Mom suddenly remembered his defiance from the previous night.

"Oh, no, Jason. Remember what happened last night? You told me that you didn't have to do things even when I asked in a nice way. I don't think that would be much fun for me on the trip. You can go with us some time when I don't have to worry about that anymore. Mabel will take care of you while we're gone. Figure out a way to pay her."

Jason stayed home, paid for his own sitter, and started to think in different ways in the future when Mom made requests in a nice way.

....

Kids Who Need More Consequences Need More Positives
Dr. Charles Fay

Most folks know at least one youngster who's misbehaving and making far more mistakes than the average! With consistent doses of Love and Logic, there's great hope for these kids. In fact, many become far better prepared for success than their better behaved peers. As we often remark, the road to wisdom is paved with plenty of mistakes—and their consequences.

As they try our patience, it's often easy to forget that consequences won't work if kids view us as uncaring or mean.

It all comes down to the "10 to 1 Rule." Since it's a well-established fact that most people assign far more weight to the negative information they receive, it's smart to balance each negative with about ten positives.

Kids who more frequently misbehave need more frequent smiles, hugs, and encouragement. Most importantly, they need to know that we care for them even when we don't care for their behavior.

Thanks for reading!

Staying Calm When Your Kids Aren't
Dr. Charles Fay

I once heard that the mark of a great leader is the ability to stay calm when others aren't. Since great parents and teachers are really the same as great leaders, it makes sense that this would apply to our daily lives with kids.

But…how do we do it?

People who meet this challenge think much differently than those who don't. When the going gets tough, those who lose their cool are led astray by thoughts such as:

- My kids should never misbehave.
- This is horrible for me.
- I'm a lousy parent (or teacher)!
- I can't help but get mad about this!

People who keep their cool are comforted by much different thoughts:

- They're sure going to learn a lot from this mistake!
- This is pretty sad for them.

- Now I get to use my new skills!
- It's okay for me to be happy even when my kids aren't.

The great news is that each of us has the power to choose how we think!

Thanks for reading!

When Kids Get in Trouble at School
Dr. Charles Fay

Parents often ask, "What should I do when my child gets in trouble at school? Should I also provide some type of consequence at home?"

An easy way to think about this is to ask yourself, "Has my child's misbehavior at school drained any of my energy?"

Sometimes the answer is clearly, "No."

When this is the case, it's often smartest to simply support the school in its choice of consequence and allow home to be a bit of a sanctuary for your child. How would you feel if your spouse gave you some sort of consequence for a mistake you made a work?

Sometimes, though, our children's misbehavior at school really does drain our energy or affect us in some direct way.

When this happens, provide some type of logical consequence:

This is so sad. I spent an hour of time and five gallons of gas driving to the school to talk to your teacher about your misbehavior. Now I don't have the energy or the money to drive you and your friends to the movies on Saturday. Now we have to stay home.

Thanks for reading!

Why TVs Don't Belong in Kids' Rooms
Dr. Charles Fay

Just a few days ago, a couple asked, "Our son wants a TV in his room. What do you think?"

"It's not a great idea," I answered.

"But what if he's a nice, responsible kid?" they prodded.

"It's not a great idea," I answered again.

There are no real benefits to allowing a TV in your child's bedroom, but there are plenty of downsides:

- Your child might develop a closer relationship with the TV than the family
- The odds go up that your child will suffer from obesity
- The odds go down that your child will get enough mental exercise
- Your child will come to believe that life is always exciting and that having to wait for anything is unfair
- It's difficult to supervise a screen that's behind closed doors
- Your child might come to believe that it's okay to act like the kids he or she sees on TV
- And so on

Should kids have TV's in their rooms? We don't think so. Thanks for reading!

Creating a Family Mission Statement
Dr. Charles Fay

In today's hectic, complicated world, many families find themselves without a "road map" for helping their kids avoid getting lost.

Might it be wise to sit down as a family and create a type of family mission statement; a set of core values that serves as a road map for behavior?

One parent described her approach:

We talked as a family about what types of values we feel proud to live by. Then we posted them on our refrigerator.
Our families believes in...

- *Treating others the way we want to be treated*
- *Honesty*
- *Politeness*
- *Doing our best even when something is hard or boring*
- *Being healthy and safe*

Our three year old needed a lot of help with these, but the older kids caught on quickly. We made sure to admit that we, as parents, would be held accountable for living by these values too!
    This is a great tool for teaching self-discipline and problem-solving. Now we just say to our kids, "Feel free to do what you would like as long as it fit our family's values."

Thanks for reading!

....

Don't Forget the Empathy!
Dr. Charles Fay

What's the very most important skill in Love and Logic?
    That's an easy one for us to answer: Empathy is the key! Without it coming first, consequences won't work.
    Empathy is like a high priced sports car—it's powerful but it needs lots of maintenance.
    Empathy's also like brightly colored clothes—it tends to fade in the wash.
    The most successful Love and Logic folks make it easier to maintain their empathy by memorizing and using just one brief empa-

thetic statement. They also make it more natural by picking one that fits their personality. Listed below are some examples:

- How sad
- Oh, no
- Dang
- That stinks
- What a bummer
- That's no good
- Awe, man

The most successful students of Love and Logic also know that how we say our empathy is far more important than what we say. Actions always speak louder than words.

Thanks for reading!

Bedroom Time
Jim Fay

When I give an evening speech I have a hard time going to sleep right away. The adrenaline level in my body has to dissipate before I can sleep. When kids go full blast until bedtime they have the same trouble.

Parents who complain that their children have a sleep problem often discover the problem is that they are expecting their kids to make an abrupt switch from a high activity level to sleep. It is better for a child to slow down and then switch from "bedroom time" to sleep time.

Reduce the level of stimulation as bedroom time approaches. Reduce the noise level in the home. Replace excitement with soothing music and remember that it is difficult for anyone to make an abrupt change from a high activity level to settling down and going to sleep.

Wise parents don't negotiate with kids about bedroom time. They know it is morally, legally, and psychologically sound to expect children to go to their rooms at a certain time every night. They know this does not damage a child's psyche or self-concept. It is healthy for families to have a scheduled "rest time" for parents and "bedroom time" for children.

....

Avoid "If-Thens" With Strong-Willed Kids
Dr. Charles Fay

It seems that just about every family has at least one child who spends most of his time trying to figure out what others want so that he can do exactly the opposite.

Frustrated by their testy behavior, it's pretty darn easy to fall into less than effective parenting practices. I hear some of these at the grocery store:

- If you're really good, then I'll buy you a candy bar.
- If you don't stop that, then you're going right to your room when we get home!

When parents are unsuccessful with strong-willed kids it's frequently because they've issued an "if-then." When their spirited kids hear this, they think, "Now the fight's on! I'll show them!"

Ironically, stubborn kids are willing to receive consequences and miss out on rewards, if it means winning a control battle.

When rewards come as a surprise to kids, they have no opportunity to sabotage themselves before they receive them. When we avoid warning them of specific consequences in advance, they spend less time fighting us and trying to figure out how to find the "loop holes" in our plans.

Thanks for reading!

....

It's Far Too Easy to Focus on the Negative
Dr. Charles Fay

I'm guilty! That's right. I've been spending too much time focusing on what others do wrong. I've slipped into zeroing in on weaknesses, instead of setting my sights on strengths.

Now I'm even focusing on how negative it's been to be negative.

Have you noticed how easy it is to fall into this trap? Is it just me, or do other folks have this problem too? It seems that most human beings tend to put more weight on negative information rather than positive. The nightly news report is a good example.

Fortunately, there's this little thing called free will. I can choose to focus on the good, instead!

Flowers need the warmth of the sun to bloom. Relationships, with kids and adults, need the warm glow of positives to blossom. In fact, most experts agree that relationships remain healthy only when each negative is balanced by ten positives.

I better get my act together! Maybe it would be wise for me to write down some of the great things I see in others and share these things with them.

It's easy to focus on the negative, but it's far more rewarding to see the positive!

Thanks for reading!

A Great Reminder
Jim Fay

This week's tip comes in the form of a note we received from Larry Anderson, who works in the South Dakota State Penitentiary.

Dear Jim,

Your article in the July issue of the Love and Logic Journal, "Immune From Responsibility," is on the mark! I have heard that story over and over again here at the pen. One 18-year-old's line was, "I only carried the gun. After they found out it wasn't loaded it shouldn't have been such a big deal."

He won't be eligible for parole until he's in his thirties. His parents had bailed him out of every scrape while he was a juvenile. He believed he couldn't be touched by consequences.

I always ask guys in my classes what it was like growing up. Their most common response is neglect. The second most common one is abusive, and then comes "helicopter" parents.

You called it the way it is.

Thanks,
Larry

....

It's Ok to Say No
Dr. Charles Fay

"Is it really ok to say no to my child?"

In the mid 1960's a few parenting "experts" began to question whether we ought to say this word to our children. Some worried that it would damage kids' self-concepts. Others seemed concerned that it would stifle creativity.

Kids need to hear "No" from time to time.

Listed below are some practical guidelines:

- **Say "No" only when you can back it up with meaningful actions.**
  When we say "no" without holding our children accountable, we teach them that "no" really means "yes."
- **Say "No" only when you can do so without anger and frustration.**
  Challenging kids love to see our faces turn red!
- **Say "No" only when it doesn't rob your child of a good learning experience.**
  If a child is about to do something that's not dangerous, but

will backfire for them, it's often wiser to allow them to learn from their mistake instead of saying "No."
- **Say "No" as often as necessary yet as infrequently as possible.** "No" is a critically important parenting tool that wears out if it's used too often. Save it for times it's really needed.

Thanks for reading!

The Gift of Giving

Jim Fay

With the holidays just around the corner I'm reminded of a story a mother told me many years ago.

While at the bank she overheard the manager talking about a project his staff was involved in. They were collecting gifts for children in the community who, without their help, would not receive anything. So far they were not doing too well. She asked what she could do to help.

At dinner she told her family about the project. With pure excitement her kids said that since they had outgrown their bikes, and were hoping for new ones from Santa, they could give their old bikes to these children.

That weekend the kids spent hours cleaning their bikes. By the time they were done, those bikes sparkled.

They delivered the bikes Monday and the look of pure joy on her children's faces made Mom's heart swell. That day they gave her a gift, too: the knowledge that she was raising kids who cared.

The holidays are a good time to remind your kids that character is more about giving than receiving.

Some Thought on Parenting With Words
Dr. Charles Fay

Those familiar with Love and Logic know that we're big on kids learning life's critical lessons by making lots of affordable mistakes and experiencing the affordable consequences of such mistakes. We're not so big on trying to teach important lessons through lectures or lots of words.

The more words we use when our kids are upset or misbehaving, the less effective we become.

With this said, there are still times when it's very important for parents to have discussions with their kids about important matters. Listed below are three little tips:

- **Have discussions only when you and your kids are calm.**
  Anger and frustration short-circuit learning—and relationships!

- **Avoid telling them things they already know.**
  A teenage client of mine complained, "My parents are always saying, 'If you don't do your home work, you're going to get bad grades.' How stupid do they think I am?"
  When we tell kids what they already know, we send the message that we don't think they are very bright.

- **Have plenty of short conversations rather than long ones.**
  Kids think the hardest about what we say when we keep our discussions short and sweet.

Thanks for reading!

School Success
Jim Fay

I've lost count of the number of phone calls I have received from frustrated educators telling about a student who appears to have no motivation for schoolwork. When I ask about the child's home life I often hear that the family is in turmoil, or that the child has few, if any, limits at home. Seldom do I hear that the child does his share of the household chores.

It is typical for the educators to say, "I know that he has a bad situation at home, but we're expected to get him to be successful at school." This is like a building contractor saying, "I know that the foundation is crumbling, but I'll guarantee to build a sturdy building anyway because that's what's expected of me."

The foundation for success in school is laid down at home with a secure home life, which includes loving limits, affection, quality time with parents, and expectations that everyone in the family does their fair share of the household chores.

The Problem With Sweet Kids

Dr. Charles Fay

Do your kids rarely argue, do what you tell them to do, and love to please you?

Yes! There are kids like this, and I'm betting that plenty of you have at least one.

While they're great fun to be around, these kids can lull us into using ineffective techniques.

I worry about sweet kids. Unlike strong-willed kids, they rarely remind us to use our Love and Logic. It's easy to stop giving enough choices. It's easy to fall back on giving orders instead of setting limits. It's easy to forget that all kids—even really compliant ones— need to make plenty of affordable mistakes.

It's not uncommon to see easy-going kids have big problems in adolescence and young adulthood. Since some haven't made enough choices and affordable mistakes, some fall prey to trying to please their peers as they have tried to please their parents.

It's not uncommon to see them get mixed up in drugs and other dangerous activities as a result.

Don't allow your sweet kids to lull you into forgetting your Love and Logic.

Thanks for reading!

....

Kids and Teachers
Jim Fay

I wonder what it would be like if all kids believed it was their job to get their teachers to like them. And all teachers believed it was their job to get kids to like them.

Do everything you can to elevate your child's teacher in his/her eyes. This is an investment you can't afford to pass up.

I know too many kids who go to school believing, "I'll be lucky if I learn anything in this lousy school." These are the kids who frequently hear critical remarks about education, the school, and the teacher. Unfortunately, kids take on the beliefs of their parents.

Don't voice these concerns in front of your kids. Deal directly with the school or with the teacher. You'll be glad you did.

....

Giving Choices Can Be Fun!
Dr. Charles Fay

I almost always do a lousy job of giving choices when I'm tired, frustrated, and trying to think of them on the spot.

Are you like me?

I've seen how much smoother life becomes when I give appropriate choices. But, for some reason, I get out of the habit.

Does this ever happen to you?

Someone gave me a gift! She walked up to me at one of my seminars and shared this little nugget of wisdom:

I make giving choices into a game for myself. It's fun when I plan ahead. First, I think, "What things will my kids try to fight me on tomorrow?" Then I look at my list. You see, I keep a list of Love and Logic choices folded up under my alarm clock. I just pick a couple. Then I imagine how much nicer my kids will act when I give these choices the next day.

It's true! Any technique is more fun and effective when we plan ahead and look forward to our kids acting up so that we can use it.

Thanks for reading!

Watchers or Doers
Jim Fay

What does your child ask when bored? Is it, "I'm bored. What can I do?" or is it, "I'm bored. What can I watch?" If it is the latter, you are raising a future watcher, not a future doer. And if this is the case, my heart goes out to your child. Becoming a watcher is not a recipe for future happiness and productivity.

Brain research shows that the brains of doers and the brains of watchers are different as a result of the way that person spends his/her time.

Do your kids a big favor and restrict electronic entertainment to 30 minutes per day. Turn your child's bedroom into a bedroom instead of a multi-media entertainment center.

Take the TV out of the child's room, and put the computer in a public area of the house. This is not illegal. It is the act of a responsible parent. If you have any doubts, read the works of researchers such as Dr. Stanley Greenspan.

When your child complains about this, answer with, "I know it's hard, but I'm your parent. It's my job."

Mastering Love and Logic
Jim Fay

I frequently hear, "I came to your seminar again because I need a shot in the arm. I've been forgetting to use my Love and Logic techniques. I guess I'm just one of those people who need to hear things several times before it becomes habit."

This is a person who knows a lot more about learning theory. The brain learns through repetition. Research tells us that we need to hear something about eight times before it locks in and starts to become part of us.

Who knows this best? Kids. Have you noticed that young children want to hear the same story over and over? Little kids know this is the best way to learn. Isn't it sad that when we grow up, we start putting ourselves down if we don't master something the very first time?

This is the reason Love and Logic material is available in audio form. The people who master the Love and Logic techniques best are the ones who listen to their favorite audio many times. When they memorize the stories, they not only have the skill, they also have the attitude and the best delivery.

....

Clues That We're Forgetting the Empathy
Dr. Charles Fay

Maybe I'm the only one who has to be reminded that nothing's more important than sincere empathy. Fortunately, others are always willing to give me some clues when I start slipping.

Do they simply spell it out in uncertain words? Do they say, "Remember to use empathy. It's the Love and Logic way!"

The clues I get are quite a bit subtler:

- I find myself in more arguments.
- The people around me seem to find all sorts of creative ways of not doing what I want. Sometimes they forget. Sometimes they comply but do a sloppier job. Sometimes they do exactly the opposite of what I ask.
- I'm frustrated and exhausted.

The most powerful way of remembering to use empathy is to memorize just one empathetic statement that fits your personal style. Listed below are some favorites:

- This is so sad.
- What a bummer.
- Oh man. This isn't good.
- Oh sweetie.

Write your favorite on little slips of paper and post them all over the house.

Thanks for reading!

Boy, Did He Dial the Wrong Number
Jim Fay

Thursday night, dinner's on the table and like clockwork, the phone rings. It's a telemarketer; well, he made it clear that he wasn't selling anything—"just a survey":

Did I think kids watched too much TV?
"Yes."

Did I think there was a lack of good family programming?
"Could be."

Did I think Hollywood had a responsibility to produce more family-friendly shows?
"I don't know if it's their responsibility."

Did I have any comments?
"Glad you asked. As a matter of fact, I do."

And so I started: "It isn't what kids watch; it's that they watch.

Kids should be reading, playing, drawing, and developing their imagination."

"Meals should never be in front of the TV; they should be a time for families to visit."

And I kept going: "Is it Hollywood's responsibility? No, it's our responsibility! TV time shouldn't be limited; it should be eliminated. We should value every moment as a family. Spend time talking, playing, sharing, and showing we care."

I took another breath, about to tell him more, but he hung up.

I hope he calls back.

....

When's It Okay to Rescue?
Dr. Charles Fay

Those who know Love and Logic know the damage done by C.H.P.S., "Chronic Helicopter Parent Syndrome."

Parents who chronically rescue their kids from the consequences of their poor decisions create kids who're chronically irresponsible and chronically unhappy. "You are so weak that you can't survive without me" is the unintentional yet very real message sent by this parenting style.

While this is true, are there any circumstances when it's okay—or essential—to rescue our kids?

Absolutely! Foster W. Cline, M.D. provides some "rules for rescue."

- Don't hesitate to rescue when life and limb are in danger.
- It's usually fine to occasionally rescue really responsible kids.
- It's typically a big mistake to rescue irresponsible ones.
- It's often okay to rescue when your child doesn't expect it.
- It's almost always unwise to rescue when your child demands it.

Good parents rescue their kids from time to time. Why? Because they realize that some day they may need to be rescued by their kids!

The great challenge for all of us is to determine whether doing so fosters love and mutual respect or dependency, resentment, and irresponsibility.

Thanks for reading!

Say "No" by Saying "Yes" to Something Else
Dr. Charles Fay

"No" seems to be the most dreaded word in the English language. Kids hate to hear it almost as much as adults! There's nothing that starts a fight faster than the simple sound of this teeny, tiny two-letter word.

The world is full of "No's." That's why preparing kids for the real world requires that we deny their requests from time to time.

But how do we say "No" without finding ourselves in constant battles? By saying "Yes" to something else!

Instead of:	No, I'm not taking you until your chores are done.
Try:	Sure! I will take you when your chores are done.
Rather than:	No. I am not paying $200 for a pair of sneakers.
Experiment with:	I want you to have those. The ones I was planning on buying cost $25. I'll provide that amount.
Instead of:	No. You are not watching rated R movies.
Try:	Renting a movie is a great idea. Find a G rated one, and we'll pop some popcorn tonight.

Give this little tip a try and enjoy fewer battles with your kids! Thanks for reading!

Mother's Day '07
Foster W. Cline

There's a special love that only mothers can show. They bestow upon their children the loving touch that seems to have a great influence on leadership development. I remember reading years ago that many, if not most, of the world's great men and women have paid tribute to their moms by giving them credit for developing their character and leadership. Our greatest general, George McArthur, was once said to have ensured that his mother was near him on his duty assignments.

Leadership is built on showing and expecting respect. A mother's love shows in many ways. Wise mothers insist on respect. Love and Logic moms always accept their child's feelings but never confuse acceptance of feelings with acceptance of disrespectful behavior. This clarity is almost perfectly designed to raise future leaders who will treat their husbands and wives with the same loving respect that their mothers encouraged and expected.

On this Mother's Day, I think of the gifts my own mother's provided. And I feel how much I miss her.

The Gift of Wisdom:

When you divide something up one kid divides, the other gets first choice.

"Be careful what you pray for. You are liable to get it!"

"Be a member of the clean plate club. Children all over the world have nothing to eat."

"I'm sure you feel that way, dear, but remember, I didn't ask for you, either."

"How can you be bored!? Find something to do!"

"I'm wondering if you would jump off a cliff because everyone else was doing it?"

Figure out which parent to ask for what, 'cause you always live by the first answer you get!

Before asking Mom for anything when the answer is liable to be "no," start with, "Mom, do you think you've done a great job and have raised a kid who can make really wise choices?"

When you are not sure what to say to your mom, shut up.

The Gift of Inquiry:

"I don't need to tell you how to spell it, look it up."

"If you can tell me before dinner why the rainbow is colored, you can have double dessert."

"When you roll your eyes up like that, can you see the bottom of your brain?"

"I bet that with a lot of thought, you can figure out why life seems unfair to you."

"Do you think you are lacking friends because you are running with a perceptive group? Check it out."

The Gift of Consequences:

After being spanked, never, never, never say, "Ha, ha, didn't hurt!"

Mom may have trouble hearing certain words that the mirror in the bedroom has no trouble accepting.

If you can't say something nice, say it to your bedpost.

You can embarrass your mom once in public. After that, you are a child of Immaculate Conception, and no one knows whose kid you are.

Mom always thought it was easier to feed a dog than a kid. So if you forgot to feed the dog, it wasn't really a problem for her.

On this Mother's Day, it is helpful to sit back and think of all the things we learned from our moms. And then, if we are lucky enough to have her still around, thank her.

When Kids Hate the Rules
By Jim Fay

"It's not fair! That dress code is bogus, man. The principal never asked the kids what they think before making that stupid rule. How can I like, express my individuality if I have to wear what the teachers like? You and some of the other moms need to do something about this!"

After a few more expletives he yells, "I bet you think the rules at that school are stupid, too. Call them and tell them I don't have to live with a lame rule like that."

This wise mom didn't fall for that. She knew that allowing kids to decide which rules they follow and don't follow is a prescription for a hard future life.

"I'm sure you see it that way, and what I think is that following their rules is probably a pain, and, I think it's in your best interest to follow them. It's no different than having to live with the stupid rules Dad and I make for the house. I'm sure you can either live with the rules or live with the consequences of not following them."

....

When Kids Say, "I'm Stupid."
Dr. Charles Fay

There are few things that tear at our hearts more than hearing our kids say, "I'm stupid."

At first glance the following parent seems to be right on track:

No you are not stupid. Honey, think of all of the things you are good at. How about reading? You're good at that! And, remember how much you improved in baseball last summer. Stupid kids don't learn how to hit curve balls like you did. And your art is wonderful. If you were dumb, would you have been able to learn how to create those drawings with such wonderful three-dimensional perspectives? I don't think so.

At second glance, we realize that this well-meaning parent is actually lending credibility to their child's "I'm stupid" remark by spending so much time and energy addressing it.

Consider employing a much simpler approach—one that avoids unintentionally reinforcing your youngster's self-deprecating remarks:

Honey, aren't you glad I don't believe that!

The most effective parents, smile, pat their child on the back, and give this sweet and simple response.

Thanks for reading!

....

Matching Funds

Jim Fay

How many kids do you know who have every new electronic gadget that comes out on the market? How many of these kids wear the latest designer fashions? How many of these kids understand how many hours their parents had to work to provide these trappings? How many of these kids believe they are entitled to the "good life" as a result of who they are? And how many of them believe the "good life" should come to those who earn it?

Entitlement is the right to demand. Great parents do not encourage this belief in their children. They expect their kids to do their fair share of the household chores and they put their kids on a matching funds program.

When Cindy's kids ask for high-priced sneakers she answers, "I'd love to see you wearing those $200.00 sneakers. My budget for shoes is $35.00. I'll contribute that much. As soon as you have the rest, you'll be wearing them."

Sometimes she contributes more, sometimes less, depending upon her budget and depending upon how important the purchase is to her. Her kids are learning that the good life comes to those who earn it.

Give Your Kids a Break – Let Them Do the Thinking
Jim Fay

Have you noticed more and more kids are having difficulty figuring things out for themselves? Could it be they're being robbed of the opportunity to do so?

A mom I know has helped with registration at the local high school for the past ten years. This year she saw a whole new breed of parents. Rather than the kids signing themselves up, the parents were making all of the decisions.

When the students were being assigned lockers, one dad who was there to "help" his son insisted he, the dad, did not like the location of the assigned locker. When the son said he thought it was fine Dad turned to him and said, "Shut up, you don't know what you're talking about."

This was just one of the many things this mom witnessed. She went home exhausted, and very sad: sad for a generation of kids who are being robbed of the opportunity to figure things out for themselves, and sad for our country.

When parents do all the thinking they rob kids of the opportunity to learn from their mistakes and send the message that the kids are not capable of figuring things out for them selves. Give your kids the can-do message: Let them do the thinking. When they learn from their mistakes they build character, strength, and confidence.

Putting an End to Sibling Spats
Dr. Charles Fay

At the root of sibling bickering and arguing is having more than one child. In other words, you are not alone! We recommend the following guidelines:

Whenever possible, stay out of it.

Kids frequently start these battles when their subconscious minds suggest that they aren't getting enough attention from us.

Let's teach our kids that this just isn't the best way to get that attention.

Ask them to take it some place, wait for later, or stay away from each other.

Unfortunately, we cannot make our kids love each other and get along. All we really have control over is being a great model and setting limits.

Have an "Energy Drain" when their fighting hassles your eyes and ears.

When our kids refuse to honor our requests, it's time to say, "This is such a bummer, guys. All of this fighting is draining my energy. How are you planning to replace that energy?"

Kids can replace our energy by doing extra chores, staying home instead of being driven some place they want to go, paying for a babysitter so that we can go out, etc.

Thanks for reading!

....

Forced Apologies
Jim Fay

As a child, Tom was very self-centered. He changed his ways only after experiencing some very hard lessons. As an adult, Tom decided he didn't want his own child to repeat his ways.

To Tom's disappointment, little Tyrone is a strong-willed, stubborn kid who never admits to being wrong. He especially gets defiant when his dad demands that he apologize for his actions.

It makes sense to Tom that learning to apologize is important for Tyrone, since that is something he himself never did as a child. However, it would be a good guess that as a child, Tom was self-centered not because he didn't apologize, but because he was not held accountable for his actions.

Unfortunately, a forced apology is worse than no apology. We learn to apologize by seeing our loved ones model it. Let your kids see you apologize frequently. And make sure they get to overhear you tell another adult how much better apologizing makes you feel.

Kids are a lot better at remembering the things they think they aren't supposed to hear, rather than what they think we want them to hear.

Is It Okay to Be Happy When Others Aren't?
Dr. Charles Fay

There are few things harder for me than seeing others upset. How about you?

Do you also find yourself getting upset when others are?

If so, pat yourself on the back. I believe that the very best parents, teachers, spouses, co-workers, etc., care deeply about the feelings of others.

Have you noticed that our greatest strengths can also become our greatest weaknesses? Maybe we have something in common. Have you ever worked so hard to make everyone happy that you've made everyone upset? Have you ever spent so much time trying to solve other people's problems that you find yourself anxious and exhausted?

Some parents spend so much time trying to keep their kids happy that they ensure them a lifetime of unhappiness.

Those of us who care about others have a major challenge: remembering that it's okay to be happy when others are not.

Healthy people aren't happy *because* others aren't. They just know that to be truly caring requires the following: empathy, allowing others to experience their own ups and downs, and allowing others to solve their own problems.

Thanks for reading!

Sabotaging Discipline

Jim Fay

Jeffery's mom complained to her Love and Logic facilitator, "Nothing works with that child. I've tried everything you taught me, but he just doesn't care. He just keeps interrupting me while I'm on the phone! I used the Energy Drain technique, but it didn't work either!"

Her skillful Love and Logic facilitator asked an insightful question: "Were you angry when you used the technique?"

"Well, of course I was. He makes me so mad. I told him that he was getting on my last nerve, and that I was sick and tired of his attitude, and that if he kept it up I was going to have some major energy drains, and that he'd better start showing a little respect around here."

So there you have it. Mom sabotaged her discipline attempt with the two things that will ruin any attempt to use Love and Logic.

She used anger instead of empathy.

She used far too many words.

All she needed to say was, "How sad. Your actions caused me an energy drain. You can put that energy back by raking the yard. Thank you."

Thanks for reading. If you like this, get your friends on board!

When to Discipline

Jim Fay

I met a man on the airplane who passed on some great advice. He said that he memorized the following rhyme. It played in his head many times as he raised his family. He said that every time he forgot to apply this wisdom he was disappointed with how he handled a situation.

Here it is:

"Never discipline in anger.
Never discipline in haste.

Save it for some happy day,
When both are feeling great."

One of the essential skills of Love and Logic parents is to delay discipline long enough to cool down, think it over, seek advice if necessary, and deliver the consequence when both the adult and child are in the thinking mode.

Hear examples of this technique on the audio CD, "Developing Character in Teens." This presentation is all about raising kids so that they will have character when they become teens. It includes examples for children of all ages.

The Power of What Kids Overhear
Dr. Charles Fay

Have you ever noticed how kids' ears tend to shrink when we try to tell them something really important? Have you also noticed how these very same ears swell when we are trying to have a private conversation with another adult?

It's a basic fact of human nature. People just have the hardest time ignoring conversations that are happening around them. We can take advantage of this fascinating phenomenon by talking about the key things we want our kids to learn—just within their hearing distance.

The more our kids overhear us talking about how we are proud to act honestly, the more likely they'll act honestly.

The more they overhear us talking about our own love of learning, the more interested in learning they will become.

The more positive comments they overhear us making about their schools and their teachers, the more respectful and motivated they will be around their schools and their teachers.

My father never tried to talk me into studying psychology, becoming an author, and teaching Love and Logic. Instead I overheard him time and time again talking about how much he loved doing these things.

Thanks for reading!

Higher Test Scores
Dave Funk

In a study mentioned by Daniel Goleman in his classic book "Emotional Intelligence", researchers studied two sets of young kids. One group was able to delay gratification, the other satisfied their wants right away. All of the kids had a choice about a tasty marshmallow set before them. When the experimenter left the room, they could eat the treat if they wanted, but if they waited until the researcher returned, they would get two. Some kids ate the marshmallow almost immediately while others waited. To be sure, waiting was hard and many stared longingly, and some sat on their hands. One kid even licked the table!

These students were studied through high school. One interesting finding was that, as a group, the kids who could wait had significantly lower incidents of drug use and delinquency. Another conclusion was that the ability to delay gratification out-ranked IQ as a predictor of high SAT scores.

Wise parents and teachers can take heart. When kids' wants, whims, and demands are not simply given in to, they learn they can survive the struggle and that life will be the better for it. Teaching kids to wait is a good lesson for life.

Avoid Using "I'm Sorry" As Your Empathetic Response
Dr. Charles Fay

Those of you familiar with Love and Logic know that the most important skill we teach is empathy. When we can provide a strong and sincere message of caring before we deliver a consequence, the child is able to focus more on the connection between their poor decision and this consequence than on anger toward us.

Those familiar with Love and Logic also know that this is not always an easy thing to do! That's why we recommend picking just one empathetic statement and memorizing it.

Some well-meaning people use "I'm sorry" as their statement. We don't recommend this. Why?

- It provides an open door for kids to argue with us by saying, "No you're not!"
- Kids can reason, "If she's apologizing for giving me this consequence, she must think she's doing something wrong."
- "I'm sorry" takes ownership of the problem rather than handing back to the child.

If you've fallen into the habit of saying, "I'm sorry," experiment with one of the following instead:

- This is so sad.
- How sad.
- What a bummer.
- Man. This stinks.

Thanks for reading!

....

There's No Need to Battle Over Homework
Dr. Charles Fay

Some of you already know that I really struggled in school as a kid. Doing what they thought was best, my parents sat right next to me and employed a combination of begging, pleading, bribing, lecturing and threatening. The harder they worked, the less I did!

When I started the fifth grade, they began a new plan that radically changed my life and theirs. We've seen similar results with family after family over the past thirty years.

Just a small part of the plan included:

- Setting aside a time and place for me to learn
- Telling me that I could either do my work or learn by thinking about it

- Saying that they would help me only as long as we didn't start arguing
- Telling me that they would help only as long as I worked harder than they did
- Allowing me to take total responsibility for my homework

Most importantly, they transferred all of the energy they had wasted fighting with me on making sure that I was respectful, did my chores, and knew that I was loved regardless of the grades I earned. Although I did worse in the short term, things really got better in the long term!

If your heart is being torn out by battles with your child over homework:

- Watch our DVD, *Hope For Underachieving Kids*
- Attend one of our one-day seminars in a city near you.

Thanks for reading!

It Takes Wisdom
Jim Fay

Jeremy, a recent business school graduate, got his dream job. He did so well that he was invited to a retreat with the big shots of the company. Not only did he get to attend, but he also had a chance to rub elbows with the top man, the CEO of the company.

Almost jittery, he approached his idol. "Sir, I was told that I could ask you a question. And what I want to ask is what it takes to become as successful as you?"

"Well, young man. Success like mine takes a whole series of good decisions."

"Oh, sir, I'm sure that's true, but what does it take to make those good decisions?"

"Well, here's that hard part, son," the older man responded with pride. "It takes wisdom."

"Oh, thank you, sir. But that creates a burning question for me. How do you acquire such wisdom?"

"Bad decisions, son. It takes a whole lot of bad decisions. Wisdom comes from learning from your mistakes."

The authors of Love and Logic meet many parents who are afraid for their kids to make the poor decisions it takes to gain wisdom about how the real world works. I hope you are not one of those parents. But if you are, this gentle reminder comes from my heart. Bruised knees and bruised emotions are the building blocks of wisdom and personal strength. Don't steal that from the kids you love so much.

Logical Consequences versus Punishment
Dr. Charles Fay

All effective parenting approaches emphasize the importance of logical consequences instead of punishment. While punishment sometimes results in quick behavior change, its side effects far outweigh its benefits. These side effects include anger, resentment, revenge, avoidance, etc.

So, how do I know if I'm using a logical consequence or a punishment with my child? The first step involves being honest with yourself as you ask the following questions:

- Am I providing this discipline to help my child learn something that will help him become a more responsible and happy individual?
- Or am I doing this to get even with my child or show him how powerful I am?

Kids are amazingly good at sniffing out our unstated intentions or goals. If we say to a child, "I'll take you the places you want to go when I feel respected," and our true goal is to help them learn, this will come through in our voice and in our body language.

If we say the same thing, but our true intention has more to do with revenge than teaching, the result will be much less positive.

Effective parents know that it's okay to delay consequences until they are ready to teach rather than punish.

Thanks for reading!

....

Manners Matter
Dr. Charles Fay

Maybe you've also noticed that manners seem to be a rare commodity these days. What a great opportunity for your kids! Since the rarer the commodity the more valuable it becomes, we can give our children a powerful advantage in the workforce, and in life, if we teach them. Listed below are some tips:

Model good manners.
What a bummer. This is the hardest part for me!

Set enforceable limits on behavior by describing what you will do or allow.
"We will stay at the restaurant as long as you guys can sit in your chairs, use quiet voices, and follow directions," is an example of an enforceable limit.

Follow through with empathy and logical consequences.
One mother wasn't afraid to get serious:

I'd been practicing table manners with my three ADHD boys, and I decided to take them out for a practice session. As soon as we ordered our meals, they started acting horrible. I guess they didn't believe I'd do anything about it. I said, "How sad, we need to go," and I took them right home. Now they get frequent compliments from others when we go out in public. The cost of that uneaten meal was sure worth it!

Thanks for reading!

Have a Perfectly Imperfect Christmas
Jim Fay

What was your best Christmas as a kid? Was it the one where there was a lot of stress about a perfect meal elegantly served—on time—to a perfectly dressed family? Or was it the one where the dog pulled the turkey off the stove and dragged it away through the dog door? There was no perfect meal that day. Everyone rolled with the punches. They rolled up their sleeves and worked together in the kitchen to salvage a makeshift meal.

The beauty of that memory is not in perfection and organization, but in remembering the joy of being together and doing things together. It was the laughter. It was one of those days when the choices were to laugh or to cry, so you all laughed it off and enjoyed one another. It brought you all together in a different way.

Holidays are times for enjoying one another. We are not suggesting that you purposely feed the turkey to the pets, but we strongly suggest that an imperfect day with little stress will create better memories of loving relationships.

We wish you a perfectly imperfect holiday season.

......

Everything Rests on Relationships
Dr. Charles Fay

What makes Love and Logic work? Some believe it's our strong emphasis on setting limits. They think that folks who are struggling with their kids just aren't setting enough limits. Others believe that the power of Love and Logic has more to do with providing consequences for misbehavior. They think that those who're unsuccessful with kids just need to do a better job of providing bigger and more powerful consequences.

Both of these viewpoints are right—and also wrong. Limits are critical, but we'll never make them stick if we don't have good relationships with our kids. Holding youngsters accountable for their misbehavior is also essential, but have you noticed that kids just don't seem to care that much about consequences when they come from someone they don't love and respect?

Everything rests on relationships. Limits gain their power from them, and so do consequences. So, if we want Love and Logic to have its full power, we're wise to do plenty of the following:

- Focus mostly on our children's strengths rather than their weaknesses.
- Smile at them as often as possible.
- Write them little notes that tell them how much we adore them.
- Greet them each day with a hug or a high five.
- Make sure that they overhear us talking about how much we love them.
- Deliver our Love and Logic with great empathy and sincerity.

Thanks for reading!

Is Your Family a Team?
Jim Fay

Please tell me this doesn't happen in your family.

Following our recent blizzard, the service and product providers known as fathers were out trying to clear the walks and driveways. There was not a kid to be seen anywhere.

I commented to a neighbor that in the past, kids would be out with their shovels helping clear the snow. After that they would be off shoveling walks to earn money.

"Is that where your kids are?" I asked.

"No," he answered. "Kids today aren't that motivated."

He blames today's kids. Little does he know that parents are the ones who train kids to believe they are honored guests in the home, rather than contributing members of a family team.

Many tasks, like snow removal or yard work, are family jobs where kids can and should become part of the team. Kids should be helping in any way that is appropriate for their age. Even small kids can help prepare drinks or snacks to serve the ones who are doing the hard work. The last thing I want to see is a kid sleeping in or playing video games while their parents do these jobs alone.

You Don't Need to Apologize
Jim Fay

After several discussions about the dangers of giving out any personal information on the Internet, Mom designed her own secret email address pretending to be an older boy. To her amazement she was able to contact her own daughter, who not only gave out her personal information, but sent a picture. All of this was in violation of the house rules for use of the Internet.

Mom told her daughter what happened. She didn't apologize for checking on the daughter, and restricted use of the computer to times when she could supervise.

Dad told Mom that she was wrong, saying that Mom had broken trust and was establishing an unhealthy mother–daughter relationship.

Mom argued, "I want her to trust that when we set rules, that we will be checking to see that they are followed. It's not unhealthy for a child to know that parents are strong enough and care enough to follow through."

Dad was dead wrong. Avoidance doesn't breed trust.

Mom was dead right. Parents shouldn't be afraid to establish themselves as the leaders of the home and as helping kids stay out of harm's way.

Hone your parenting skills with the updated *Parenting With Love and Logic* books.

Is "I'm Sorry" Enough?
Dr. Charles Fay

I'm asked quite often, "When my child misbehaves or causes a problem for someone, he's quick to say, 'I'm sorry.' Is that enough, or should he have a consequence?"

Common sense tells us that actions speak louder than words. That's why it's important that our kids do more than just apologize. Let's take a look at an example:

Parent: This is so sad. You rode your bike right through Mrs. Wilson's flowers. What are you going to do?
Child: Uh, say 'I'm sorry'?
Parent: That's a great start! What can you do to show her that you are sorry?
Child: I don't know.
Parent: Would you like to hear some ideas?
Child: What?
Parent: Some kids decide to buy some new flowers and plant them for her. How would that work?
Child: I don't have any money.
Parent: Other kids ask their parents to buy some new flowers, and they pay their parents back by doing lots of extra chores. Let me know what you decide. Good luck.

That's Love and Logic.
Thanks for reading!

When Children Overeat
Dr. Charles Fay

More parents are concerned about their children's overeating. One mom put it this way: "Our eleven-year-old is a really sweet and responsible kid, but he sneaks out of his room to eat. He's starting to get teased at school about his weight."

Dealing with eating issues can be complex, so I recommend that concerned parents get professional help. I also suggest the following:

- **Discuss how some people overeat in an attempt to sooth emotional hurts.**

   Do you know that some kids eat too much of the wrong things because they feel really bad about stuff in their lives? They get confused and start thinking that the hurts they feel in their heart are hunger pangs. Sometimes school isn't going well, they are getting picked on, etc. Kids who have these problems find that they aren't so hungry when they talk about their hurts with someone nice.

- **Expect them to pay for the food they eat in between meals.** This is not done out of punishment. It's conducted as a simple non-emotional business transaction:

   The healthy food I serve for meals is free. I'll just take the cost of the extra food you eat out of your allowance.

Thanks for reading!

....

Thanks, Mom
Jim Fay

"Mom — I just had to call and tell you that I got a new assignment at work and now I have to supervise and train all the new hires. I'm really enjoying it, but I can't believe how irresponsible some of these young people are. They can't get to work on time and they keep taking days off when they don't feel like working.

"I think I got this job because I'm not like that. But I think I might have ended up just like them if you hadn't turned me around. I still remember how mad I was at you when you did it. I told you that it was because of that stupid Love and Logic class you were taking. Now I know it was the best thing you ever did for me.

"Remember when I was in the band and we traveled to the band contest? I forgot my uniform shoes and called you and told you to bring them right away.

"I'll never forget what you said. You told me that it was 'Grow up time.' We lost because I didn't have the right uniform and I was furious at you.

"The only thing I can say now is THANK YOU!"

Learn more on our updated, *Parenting Teens With Love and Logic*.

....

The Gift of Struggle

Dr. Charles Fay

Most little kids reach a certain point at which they want to do many things without our help. They want to feed themselves, they want to open every door without assistance, they want to button their buttons, etc. If we try to help, we often hear, "No! Me!" While frustrating for everyone, this stage is important. Little ones know down deep that they need to experience struggle to learn.

As our kids grow, many of us forget that struggle is a gift. When they are having a hard time tying their shoes, we quickly do it for them. When they are challenged with homework, we too often jump in and tell them how to do it. It's hard to sit back, watch, and allow them to learn through repeated effort.

In our CD, *Shaping Self-Concept*, you will hear that kids learn to feel good about themselves when they are allowed to struggle and experience the resulting pride of accomplishment.

When your kids are struggling with something, experiment with saying, "I bet you can figure that out. If you don't get it by _____, then I'll give you some ideas."

And when you do help, remember the following rule:

Never work harder than your child.

Thanks for reading!

The Importance of Thankfulness
Dr. Charles Fay

I remember it well. It was my tenth birthday, and my great grandfather had just given me a new fishing rod and reel. Without thinking, I ran out onto the lawn and started catching imaginary five-pound Rainbow trout out of my mother's flower garden.

In my state of euphoria, I'd forgotten to thank him for my gift. Like a lightning bolt my mother shot out of the house, screen door smacking behind her. "What did you forget to say?" she asked with loving authority.

I was lucky enough to grow up in a home where three words were modeled and always expected. Two of them were "Thank you" and the third was "Please." We heard them use these words a lot. They used them with each other, with other adults, and with us.

We learned early on that forgetting these words meant certain disapproval and potentially very sad consequences. As a result they became a habit.

Are your kids developing this habit? If not, it's never too early to start. Thanks for reading!

"I'm Bored, What Can I Watch?"
Jim Fay

I was raised in an era when kids knew that it was their responsibility to entertain themselves. When we got bored we asked, "What can we do?" If your kids ask this question, you are doing a good job of parenting.

Many kids today ask, "I'm bored. What can I watch?" This is difficult to combat in an era where television and video games can keep kids in an almost constant state of stimulation.

Research on the brain tells us that this constant excitement can wire a kid's brain to prefer activities that offer immediate stimulation and entertainment. As a result we see many children who cannot handle the slower speed of a normal classroom. These kids see school as boring and often stimulate themselves by acting out.

Our media-driven culture of constant stimulation through TV and video games contributes to the number of kids who need and demand instant gratification. Dr. Ed Hallowell describes these kids as attention-disordered.

Do your kids a favor and limit the amount of time their brains are connected to electronic entertainment. More than one-half hour per day is hurtful to your child's brain.

Learn more about hyperactive children in *Meeting the Challenge* by Jim Fay and Dr. Bob Sornson.

You Don't Have to Be a Perfect Parent
Dr. Charles Fay

Do you ever find yourself feeling angry or frustrated and slipping into less-than-effective parenting practices? Despite my very best intentions, there are times when I just don't handle things as well as I think I should. When this happens, I find it hard not to feel discouraged. Fortunately, you don't have to be a perfect parent to raise really great kids! Your kids need to see you struggle. When they see you stumble a bit, pick yourselves back up, learn from your mistakes, and never give up, they learn to do the same.

While my own parents made their fair share of blunders, they never stopped learning and they've never stopped growing. Little did they know that they were doing what research shows is the most effective. Yes! The great psychologist, Albert Bandura, observed that children are far more likely to learn from imperfect "coping models" than those who never struggle or make mistakes.

The key is showing your kids that you are always learning. The most successful parents keep reading and listening to Love and Logic over and over. This repetition helps lock in the learning. A new, fun and FREE way to do this is by visiting the Dr. Fay Show on our website. Just click on the old-fashioned microphone and listen to my weekly radio show/podcast.

Thanks for reading!

....

Friends...When Our Kids Pick Ones We Don't Like
Dr. Charles Fay

Rather than fighting a losing battle over who our kids choose as friends, we're far wiser to focus on upping the odds that our young-sters will make good decisions, even when their buddies don't. Listed below are three quick tips:

Send strength messages.
"Hanging around Joe is going to get you in trouble," sends the message that your child is too weak to think for himself.

"It's a good thing that Joe has a friend like you who makes good decisions," tells your child that he can think for himself.

Talk about the friend's *behavior* rather than the friend.
Talking with your child about how "bad" a friend is implies that your child is bad for choosing them.

Wiser parents talk about the types of sad consequences a friend's irresponsible behavior might bring about.

Allow your child to use you as the "bad guy."
Experiment with saying:

If your friends ever pressure you to do something you don't think is right, feel free to blame me for your not going along with them. You might just say, "My dad is so crazy, you never know what he will do."

Thanks for reading!

Don't Use Pets to Teach Responsibility
Dr. Charles Fay

Have you ever heard someone say, "We're buying Toby a dog, so that he can learn some responsibility"? I'm not sure where and when it got started, but this notion of using pets in an attempt to teach responsibility seems to be growing in popularity. I wonder how many thousands of pets have suffered as a result.

Pets should be used to reward proven responsibility rather than being used to teach it.

When children prove they can remember to take out the trash, shovel snow from the sidewalk, put their dirty clothes in the hamper, and other chores, then we know that they're ready for a pet.

If your child is doing a poor job of taking care of a pet you already own, there are two options. First, you may consider finding another home for the animal. Second, you may decide to take care of the pet yourself and have your child do some of your chores in exchange.

Thanks for reading!

The Path to Positive Self-Concept
Dr. Charles Fay

Over the past three decades, psychologists have placed huge emphasis on the importance of having a positive self-concept. Rightly so! How we feel about ourselves may be the single most important factor affecting how motivated we are to succeed in school, the types of friends we select, the person we marry, etc.

Due to its undisputed importance, people have spent tremendous energy trying different approaches to give kids good self-concepts. Listed below are just a few of the many tactics that have created selfish kids rather than ones with a good sense of self:

- Constant praise
- Ensuring that they are always the center of attention
- Making sure that they never encounter any hardships
- Buying them everything they want
- Rescuing them from the consequences of their misbehavior
- Setting no limits so that they can "express their creativity"

There's only one approach that really works, and it's based on the following age-old truism:

The best way to feel good is to do something good.

When parents place a high emphasis on good and respectful behavior, children look at themselves and think, "I act pretty darn good and responsible. I must be pretty darn good and responsible."

True self-concept is developed when children encounter struggles, are taught how to overcome these struggles, and see themselves acting in respectful and responsible ways. Stated quite simply, self-concept is an inside job.

Thanks for reading!

You Can't Make Someone Mad and Sell Them Something at the Same Time
Jim Fay

Sonya recognized me in the airport. She approached me saying, "My friend gave me an audio CD called 'Love and Logic Magic

When Kids Drain Your Energy.' Now all I have to do is put my hand on my forehead and the oldest one tells his brother to shape up 'because Mom's fixin' to have an energy drain.' It works great!"

"I'm glad it's working for you," I replied.

"Oh, it is," she said, "But now I have to get my husband to buy into Love and Logic."

I was quick to say, "Please don't try to sell Dad on Love and Logic. Telling someone that they are wrong is not usually a good selling technique.

Dad might become interested in what you are doing if he sees you being successful with the kids. Tell Dad that he should parent in his own way and that you want to experiment with the Love and Logic techniques to see if it makes your own job easier. Listen frequently to your CD's when he might accidentally hear them. The odds for success are always better when someone buys in on their own, just as you did."

Raising Children Who Don't Need Us
Dr. Charles Fay

I've learned over the years that the best way to get a crowd of parents to gasp in shock is to tell them that their most important job is to raise kids who don't need them. While tough for some of us to choke down, this may be the single most telling important distinction between successful and not-so-successful parents.

Love and Logic is devoted to helping parents raise kids who want to be around them, but don't need to be around them. Wouldn't it be great if your grown kids called you up and said, "Mom and Dad, let's get together!" instead of "Mom and Dad, I need some cash!"

On a daily basis, the most effective parents ask themselves, "What can I do today that will help my kids become more independent than they were yesterday?" "What can I teach them that will allow them to rely just a bit more on themselves, and just a bit less on me?"

A basic human need is to be needed. Really healthy parents are very careful not to use their children to meet this need. Instead, they find other ways to feel needed while giving their kids the priceless gift of knowing that they've got what it takes to be independent and successful.

Thanks for reading!

······

An Open Letter from Dr. Foster Cline to America's Moms
Foster W. Cline, M.D.

Boy, does America owe you!! Have a great day. But, you know, celebrating Mom on only one special day of appreciation trivializes the massive contributions, sacrifices and energy that all of you offer America's kids day in and day out. Actually, appreciation should be automatic everyday when children are raised with Love and Logic's three goals of being responsible, respectful, and fun to be around.

Every day should be a day of celebrating what parents do for kids (and vice versa) and it takes away from that expectation to have a "special day" when cards and flowers are given. Of course, every florist and every card maker promotes the "special day," but wouldn't every one of you be flabbergasted and overjoyed to be given flowers or a card from kids and hubby when it is NOT a special day?

"Just 'cause I wanted to, Mom."

Well, that being said, what is great about Mother's Day?

- Mother's Day is a day you can discourage entitlement in your children. It is a special day when kids are expected to say, "Thank you." That's important in this day and age where many children may be more likely to say, "What you need to do, Mom, is pick me up at … " It is little comfort to have breakfast in bed one day a year, when the rest of the year you are in the kitchen fixing breakfast and packing lunches with nary a "thank you."
- Mother's Day can be a "wake-up call" for some of you concerning expectations. "Gosh, these kids can really be neat!" Naturally,

it would be unrealistic to say, "Wow, now that I see how you are coming through today, I think I'll expect such massive gratefulness every day!" But it might be a good idea to vibrate out the expectation that some of the day's massive amount of grateful expressions could spill over to the rest of the year.

- When children show appreciation toward you, it raises their self-image. Why is that? It's because kids put their parents inside themselves as their identification figure, inner self, ego-ideal, role model or whatever you want to call it. So when kids show they feel good about you, and you love them, and part of you lives inside of them, then your children feel good about themselves. All disrespectful children of loving parents have a poor self-image. Respectful, loving children who do good things for their parents have a high self-image and do good things for themselves. This essential concept, the way kids treat parents, is a reflection of how they treat themselves, and is pretty eye-opening.

Finally, there is a related concept. You might profitably use Mother's Day as a day of reflection and goal setting.

- What are my true expectations for "thank you" from the children?
- How do I hope my children will grow over the next year? How will they be different a year from now?
- If I do hope they are different, what can I do over the next twelve months to facilitate that?

And of course, Mother's Day can be a day where it is "legal" and not strange for Moms to ask:

- Hey, guys, tell me what you appreciate most about me.
- Can you think of any way that I could be an even better Mom?
- Could you tell me what I did that made you happiest over the last year?

So, Moms, soak up your special day. But what the heck, you might as well use it effectively.

A Very Special Type of Gang

Dr. Charles Fay

I want every child to get heavily involved in gang activities as early in life as possible. That's right! Gangs are great for kids. That is, as long as the "gang" is the child's family.

Let me clarify. Children who feel like they are part of a gang at home are far less likely to join a gang outside of the home. Kids who feel starved for belonging, structure, the predictability of rituals, and power, will look to meet these needs wherever they can.

We can learn a lot from street gangs:

- Members are given special nicknames
- There are clear limits or rules
- Members are expected to contribute by performing specific tasks
- Traditional rites of passage are adhered to firmly

Families that provide such things seem to raise the happiest and most responsible kids. There's something about being called by an affectionate nickname that makes one feel loved and valued. Clear and consistent limits leave us feeling safe. Being expected to complete chores meets the need to be needed. Sitting together for family meals, participating in religious services, and creating unique family traditions gives us a sense of predictability and tradition.

Thanks for reading!

Are You Brave Enough for Mistakes?

Dr. Charles Fay

It takes a tremendous amount of courage to raise respectful and responsible kids! It's not easy to set and enforce limits when we know that doing so will probably make our kids really upset in the short term.

Allowing our children to make mistakes can be one of the scariest things of all. It can be scary to watch them:

- Staying up too late
- Forgetting to put away their toys
- Refusing to eat their dinner
- Forgetting to bring their homework to school
- Going outside on a cool day without their coat
- Leaving their bicycle unlocked at school
- Using their allowance to buy a toy that will surely break
- Spending all of their money on a car stereo when their car doesn't even run

In our book, *Love and Logic Magic for Early Childhood*, we teach that mistakes made early in life are far better bargains than those made later on. When we are brave enough to allow little mistakes, our children are far less likely to make really big ones.

Thanks for reading!

Have You Forgotten the Empathy?
Dr. Charles Fay

It's the simplest yet most difficult skill. It's the most powerful yet hardest to do. It makes the difference between our kids learning responsibility versus learning resentment. It's the heart of Love and Logic, and it's the key to making just about any parenting technique work.

Those familiar with Love and Logic know that I'm talking about empathy. We've all seen it in action. We've all seen how much better kids respond when we provide strong doses of sincere empathy before we prescribe consequences.

That's the Love and Logic formula: Heap on the empathy before providing the consequence.

Why is empathy so easy to forget as we go through our daily lives with our families? I don't know. It just is. One strategy for staying on track is listening to the very same Love and Logic CD over and over again. The more times you listen, the easier it is to remember, when the pressure is on. The CD, The Four Steps to Responsibility, is my personal favorite. It reminds me that kids learn from mistakes only when they know that we really love them and care.

Thanks for reading!

....

Healthy Family Communication
Dr. Charles Fay

The dysfunctional family makes great TV sitcom material, probably because we recognize many of the themes from our own childhoods, and probably because these shows leave us thinking, "What a relief. At least our family isn't as big a mess as that one!"

Dysfunctional families may be entertaining to watch on TV, but they're horribly sad to belong to. Fortunately, mental health experts have learned a great deal about how to help families operate in healthy, happy ways. One of the most helpful discoveries involves who family members talk to when a problem arises.

- In healthy families, Mom talks to Dad when she is upset with Dad.
- In unhealthy families, Mom talks to the kids when she is upset with Dad.

- In healthy families, Dad talks to Mom when he's upset with Mom.
- In unhealthy families, Dad talks to his friends when he is upset with Mom.

- In healthy families, Junior talks to Dad when he wants something from Dad.
- In unhealthy families, Junior talks to Mom when he wants something from Dad.

- In healthy families, Junior talks to his teacher when he doesn't understand an assignment.
- In unhealthy families, Mom and Dad talk to Junior's teacher when Junior doesn't understand an assignment.

I bet you see the pattern here! In the healthiest families, family members share their concerns directly with the person involved with the concern, rather than dragging a third party into the mix.

....

Don't Be Afraid to Take a Stand

Jim Fay

On page 47 of "Love and Logic's Journal Collection", Dr. Foster Cline writes, "It's sad to see the number of parents who don't take a stand with their children. They fear their children will see them as mean, unreasonable, or dictatorial. Some actually fear their children will be ruined in some way if they take a firm stand about behavior."

All of my experience says that the opposite is true. Parents who will not take a stand on behavior most often raise children who feel contempt for their folks.

Foster writes that it doesn't hurt a child in any way when a parent speaks in a firm voice. However, it is important to make sure your voice sounds firm, not angry.

Just as animals all have a way of puffing themselves up to act more ferocious when they are afraid, humans often get angry to appear stronger when they fear a loss of control.

Kids have an innate ability to sense this, seeing us as being mean and ineffective.

A firm voice saying, "Ok, guys. Take it somewhere else. You can come back when there is no bickering!" is far more effective than, "What is the matter with you. This is making me so angry!"

Find more in *Love and Logic Tenth Anniversary Journal Collection*.

....

Arguing
Dr. Charles Fay

How sad it is that so many young people in our world have come to believe that constant manipulation is the best way to get what you want!

Love and Logic offers a very powerful way of breaking kids of this damaging habit. The first step involves reminding ourselves that it's okay if our kids get upset about a limit we have set. Sometimes we have to allow our kids to be upset in the short term so that they can become responsible and happy in the long term.

The second step requires going "brain dead." The less we think about what an arguing child is saying, the more energy we'll have at the end of the day.

The third step involves calmly repeating the very same "one-liner," regardless of what the child says. Examples include:

- What did I say?
- I love you too much to argue.
- That's a good argument, but your last one was better.
- I argue at 6 a.m. on Saturdays.
- I know.

To learn more about parenting kids who love to argue, read our book, *Love and Logic Magic: When Kids Leave You Speechless.*

Thanks for reading!

The Simple Principle
Dr. Charles Fay

We can make our relationships with others really complicated, or we can keep them simple by understanding the following principle:

People continue to behave in ways that pay off for them in the short term.

If my toddler constantly screams in my ear when I'm trying to talk on the phone, I need to make sure that that behavior no longer pays off for him in the short term. Many parents find it effective to ignore the child and keep the phone up by their ear long after the other party hangs up. Without saying a word to the child, they continue the "call" until the child is finished screaming their brains out. In this way, their child learns that screaming just prolongs the length of each call.

If an adult in your life always criticizes what you do, this principle also applies. A friend of ours trained her husband by saying in a very loving way, "Honey, when you complain about dinner being a bit late, I get so sad and nervous that I find myself burning things."

It wasn't long before he realized that complaining about the timing of dinner simply resulted in a scorched dinner.

Thanks for reading!

Cell Phones
Dr. Charles Fay

More and more really good kids are getting in big trouble with cell phones.

Teachers are pulling their hair out over students who spend more time text messaging than learning. Some students are even using phones to take inappropriate pictures of test answers—and each other!

Teen drivers and cell phones create havoc—and death!

Parents are finding themselves in constant battles with their kids over huge cell phone bills, lost phones, stolen phones, damaged phones, phones being used at the dinner table and during church, phones being taken away at school, etc.

Here are some suggestions:

- Be a good model. Don't use your phone while driving, and show respect for others by turning it off when you should.
- Let your child know that they can have a phone only when they can pay for the privilege.

- Don't fall into the trap of believing that your kid has to have a phone for safety reasons.
- If the phone is lost, stolen, or taken away at school, it's gone. Don't buy them another.
- Take it away if it becomes a problem.

While this advice may seem old-fashioned, parents who follow it raise far more respectful and responsible kids.

Thanks for reading!

....

What Comes Around Goes Around

Dr. Charles Fay

Do you ever worry that your kids might grow up and spend most of their time making excuses about why they are too busy to visit or to help you when you're the most in need?

Fortunately, there's a powerful strategy that kills two birds with one stone. It creates kids who're more likely to help you when you are old, and it also creates kids who're more likely to do their chores before you get old.

The next time you see your kids working hard at one of their chores, ask them if they'd like your help. Then give them a hand as long as they continue to work at least as hard as you are. Have fun together!

One of the best ways to get children to more frequently do something you want is to pay attention to them when they're doing it. When we apply this to chores, we get a nice benefit in the short term. And grown kids who are far more willing to help us out in the long term.

Thanks for reading!

....

Love and Logic Won't Work Without the Empathy
Dr. Charles Fay

If you're like me, you find yourself gradually getting out of the Love and Logic habit. My biggest challenge is to remember the empathy. It's so easy to begin slipping. If I'm not careful, I start applying Lectures and Logic, instead of Love and Logic.

Empathy really is the key to making it all work! And it seems so simple at first glance. All I have to do is lock in a strong dose of sadness or empathy before delivering consequences. "What a bummer. You guys have been fighting over the remote control. I bet if you did some chores together, that would help you learn to cooperate." That seems easy. Or is it?

All's good and fine until the rubber hits the pavement in our own homes. In my CD, "Oh Great! What Do I Do Now?" I teach a variety of strategies for helping parents use empathy—even when they don't feel like it. One of these strategies involves saying to your child:

> *I'm going to have to do something about this—but not now—later. I make better decisions when I'm calm. We'll talk then.*

Thanks for reading!

··

The Meanest Mother in the World
Jim Fay

Dave Funk passed this along from one of his Love and Logic students. I think all kids would be lucky to have such a mean mother.

> *My son, Robert, and his girlfriend, Jenna, were here last night. Jenna asked me what I was reading, so I did a quick explanation of the updated version of Parenting With Love and Logic.*
>
> *After hearing this explanation, my son said, "So that's who is to blame!" I laughed and asked innocently what he meant. "Oh,*

*you know. When I was growing up, it was more work to get in
trouble than what it was worth." I have heard the same complaints from my daughter. She used to tell me I was the meanest
mother. I didn't yell. I didn't scold. I didn't say I told you so. I
let them know how sorry I was that they were in trouble or had
made a poor choice. Or worse, I was told, I would make them
wait until I was ready to listen. But I think what they were both
telling me was that they believed, at the time, that forcing them
to think and solve their own problems was cruel and unusual
punishment. But now that they are adults, they are both very
good problem-solvers and take ownership of their decisions.*

Dad and Shopping
Jim Fay

Marge's kids had a history of keeping her upset during shopping trips.
They ran all over the store and were frequently lost. They had trained
her to keep her eye on them to the expense of her doing her shopping.

Contrast that to my own dad, who trained his kids to keep their
eyes on him instead.

We'd enter the store and as he went through the front door of
Republic Drug he'd be saying, "Well guys, try to keep up. I'll be moving kind of fast. Hope you don't get lost, but if you do, find one of the
security guys over at that desk. He'll probably help you find a way to
get home. I've never seen a kid lost for more than a few months."

As he said this, he never looked back. Needless to say, we stayed
close. Not only did we believe that his word was good on these
shopping trips, but any other time he opened his mouth, as well.

It wasn't until years later that he admitted to us that he had
talked to the security people before he took us shopping, and these
trips were nothing but training sessions.

He was a strong believer in the idea that advance training could
save him a lot of time and frustration later.

Be Careful About Taking Away What Your Kids Need the Most
Dr. Charles Fay

When we've got a seriously underachieving youngster, it's awfully tempting to resort to taking away all sorts of things in a desperate attempt to motivate them to do their schoolwork. Sadly, this often backfires, leading the child to become even more resistant about learning.

Most of us wouldn't feel that motivated if our spouse said, "Ok, that's it! No more golf [or whatever else we might love to do] until I start getting some better reports from your boss!"

While it's entirely reasonable to set some limits on TV, video games, and other entertainment activities when kids are doing poorly in school, taking them out of their favorite sport, Boy Scouts, music lessons, etc., is a bad idea. The research is clear on this:

Children who are involved in a healthy extracurricular activity are far less likely to get involved in drugs, sex, gangs, and other high-risk activities.

Kids who are struggling in school need at least one natural high, so that they aren't so tempted by various artificial ones. For additional tips for helping underachieving kids, view our DVD titled, "Hope for Underachieving Kids".

Thanks for reading!

"Loan Me the Money"
Jim Fay

Kendra and Dad were walking through the mall when Kendra spied the most "spectacular" pair of dark glasses.

"Oh, Dad, they are perfect. They're just what I need to complete my collection of eyewear. I've got to have them, but I don't have the money. Will you loan me some? Pleeeze! I'll pay you back."

Dad knew that a loan to Kendra was never a loan. In the past, asking for re-payment drew fits and sulking. With this in mind, he knew that he had only three choices:

- Loan her the money and fight with her for re-payment.
- Give her the money and avoid all the hassle.
- Make her sign a promissory note and hope for better results this time.

But wait! Why are these his only choices? Contrary to what the media and advertising says about having it now and paying later, there is another choice. Kendra might learn more about money management and decision-making if she earns the money and buys later.

A wise father will say, "They are beautiful. I can't wait to see you wearing them. You can come back for them when you have the money."

"But, Dad. I don't know why you're so uptight about money. It's no big deal to loan it to me!"

"You're right, Kendra. A big deal is learning how to earn and manage your own money."

How to Get Kids to Lie

Jim Fay

Rex had been terrorizing the other 5th graders at school. The other kids were beginning to refuse to play anywhere near him during recess.

Rex's teacher was often convinced that he was behind most problems that happened when her back was turned. She explained it to his mother one day with, "I never see him cause a problem, but when there is one, he's the kid who knows all the details and looks more innocent than anyone else."

Finally the playground supervisor saw him punch one of the girls from behind, knocking her to the ground. However, when told about this, his mother refused to believe the story.

Her response was, "I asked Rex if he did it, and he said no. I have to believe my child."

Mom fell into a trap occupied by many parents who don't realize that it is human nature to deny responsibility. The best way to get anyone to lie is to ask, "Did you do that?"

What is the solution? Once you know something happened, don't ask your child if he/she did it. Do this instead:

"Rex. I know that you hit the girl. Here is what I'm going to do about it."

Rex will still say, "But I didn't do it."

"I'm sorry, Rex. That's not what we are talking about. We are talking about what's going to happen."

Continue to play "broken record" with this regardless of what he says. Learn more about kids and lying in, *Parenting With Love and Logic.* Thanks for reading.

Is It Okay to Have a Parenting Pet Peeve?
Dr. Charles Fay

If you're like about 99 percent of us, you have at least one thing that you feel so strongly about that you can't bear to see your kids do it. I'm not talking about huge things like sex, drugs, or gangs. It's our job to take a stand on these issues. What I'm talking about here is much littler stuff, like them making popping sounds with their gum, wearing their hats inside, rolling their eyes, saying "like" like a lot, wanting long hair, letting their rooms resemble the local landfill, etc.

There's nothing wrong with having a parenting pet peeve or two. That is, as long as you aren't attempting to micromanage or control your kids over every issue.

What's my advice? Share plenty of control in the form of small choices. "Do you want juice or milk?" or "Do you want to do your chores now or in fifteen minutes?" are good examples. In our CD *Avoiding Power Struggles With Kids*, we teach that the more choices like these you give, the more likely your child will comply when you say, "I know this may sound uptight to you, but I'd really like you to do this. Thanks!"

Thanks for reading!

....

Some Thoughts on Video and Computer Games
Dr. Charles Fay

Over the past two decades, video and computer games have become dramatically more fast-paced, realistic, and stimulating. Not long after their introduction, I began to suspect that these games had the same addictive potential as drugs, alcohol, and gambling. Today, family therapists and researchers have confirmed my fears. Listed below are some tips for helping your child avoid getting hooked:

- Don't allow your child to have a computer in his/her room.
- Allow them to play these games no longer than thirty minutes per day.
- If your child becomes sneaky, noncompliant, or defiant about this time limit, remove this privilege.
- Children birth to six should spend no time playing these games, watching videos, or viewing television.
- So-called "educational" games, videos, and shows are no substitute for real-life learning activities, involving movement, problem-solving, and human relationships.

For more information, read *Love and Logic Magic: When Kids Leave You Speechless*. You'll find plenty of practical strategies and the actual words to use with your kids.

Thanks for reading!

....

What's Our Job?
Dr. Charles Fay

When asked, "What's our job as a great parent or great teacher?" most people say something like, "To raise or help create really respectful and responsible kids." Our good friend and co-founder of Love and Logic, Foster W. Cline, M.D., disagrees. Dr. Cline argues:

> *It's not our job to raise responsible kids. Our job is to consistently do the things that give kids an opportunity to become responsible.*

When we spend all of our time and energy trying to make our kids respectful and responsible, we open ourselves up to major power-struggles. It's as if we send an unstated message such as, "All of my self-worth and happiness is tied up in how well you behave." This is far too much power for any child to have. Too often, strong-willed children use this power to punish their parents.

In contrast, when we focus on doing the right things and giving our kids a great *opportunity*, we place appropriate responsibility on them and they have no battle to fight. The unstated message is much different: "While I want very much for you to have a happy and responsible life, I can't make that happen for you. You are the one who has to do most of the work."

Take care of yourself by remembering that the only thing you really have complete control over is yourself.

Thanks for reading!

The Love and Logic Vaccination Plan
Dr. Charles Fay

Our world is getting more complex and dangerous for kids every day. How do we best protect them so that they will survive?

Resist the urge to overprotect!

Like vaccinations for physical disease, parents who apply Love and Logic allow their kids to develop decision-making "antibodies" by being exposed to plenty of small temptations, by being allowed to make plenty of small mistakes, and by being loved enough to be held accountable for their poor decisions.

It makes sense that if our child is about to run into a busy intersection or jam a fork into an electrical outlet, we're going to step in. But how do we respond when the temptations they face have much smaller, more affordable price tags?

Lucky is the child whose parents are brave enough to let them make the mistake of wasting their allowance on bubble gum. Even luckier is the child whose parents also hold him accountable by refusing to give in when he begs for more cash.

Lucky is the child whose parents are brave enough to let her make the mistake of watching TV instead of finishing her science fair project. Even luckier is the child whose parents love her enough to resist the urge to do the project for her.

Yes! Lucky indeed is the child who understands through experience that every decision has its consequences.

Thanks for reading!

··

Kids, Money, Loans
By Jim Fay

April has been declared National Financial Literacy Month. What a great time to teach your kids about loans! Many parents wonder if it is a good idea to loan money to your children.

The authors of Love and Logic say yes. If your kids will need to know about loans as adults, they need some practice with small loans.

Jan proudly told her friend that she had just repossessed a $189 camera from her son.

"Oh, that's terrible. How could you ever do that?" responded her friend.

"My son was really lucky," said Jan. "We make loans to our son just the same way the bank does it. Now, at age 12, he understands all about collateral and the responsibility of paying back his loans.

Compare that to my neighbor's 21-year-old kid. His parents always let him off the hook for his loans and he had to learn when the price was higher. The finance company just repossessed his $17,000 car. I think my child got a real bargain. Don't you?"

Keep your eyes out for my new book, co-written by Kristan Leatherman, M.S., available this summer called *Millionaire Babies or Bankrupt Brats?*. In the mean time, check out the special this week on *Parenting with Love and Logic*.

....

Raise Great Employees
Dr. Charles Fay

It's getting harder to find good, responsible employees. While a problem for employers, this provides a great opportunity for parents! If we can teach the following skills and attitudes, we can practically guarantee that our youngsters will become financially secure adults:

- The ability to complete tasks without reminders
- The desire to be proud of one's work
- Knowing how to cooperate and compromise
- The self-discipline to complete boring, tedious tasks
- Being able to creatively solve new and unique problems
- The ability to learn from one's mistakes

The single most important thing we can do to help our kids develop these skills is to expect them to complete chores without reminders and without pay. In our CD, *"Didn't I Tell You to Take Out the Trash?,"* we teach the following steps for making this happen:

- Instead of saying, "Take out the trash, now!" try giving your child a deadline, "Just have the trash taken out by six o'clock."
- This deadline gives you plenty of time to think about what you will do if your child forgets or refuses to do the chore.
- Resist the urge to nag and remind.

- If your child forgets or refuses to do the chore, do it for them.
- With great empathy, provide a consequence. "This is so sad. I did your chores. How are you planning to pay me?"
- Your child can pay by doing extra chores, staying home instead of being driven somewhere they want to go, giving you a toy, etc.

Thanks for reading!

Shopping Daze
Jim Fay

I watched a frustrated mom trying to get the weekly grocery shopping done.

She was becoming increasingly frazzled with three kids putting her through her paces. They could have been a great help. Instead they were as distracting as a swarm of bees.

Mom's head was constantly switching back and forth, paying attention to each kid who was running up to her holding bags of treats up to her face so that she could see what they wanted. They had each mastered the art of, "Look Mom," followed with the begging face and pumping body. The message was clear: "I need this right now or I will probably die before your very eyes."

She kept saying, "No. You don't need that," but was finally worn down to the point of giving in. Before long her basket had items that she never intended to buy.

Later that morning I saw another family. The kids had specific missions to find certain items for Mom. They sailed through the store in half the time.

I asked this mom how she did it and she told me her plan:

"We had several practice trips to the store. Now the kids pick their tasks from my shopping list. The kids add their treats to the list before we go and they know that we are not buying anything else.

"If they ever ask for something else, I just say, 'It's on your dime,' and they know that if I have to repeat it, their treats go off the list or out of the basket and back on to the shelves."

Get more information about kids and shopping in *The Love and Logic 10th Anniversary Journal Collection*. Read article titled "The Strategic Training Session" in Chapter 3, Volume 3.

Thanks for reading!

Easy-Going Kids Need Love and Logic, Too!
Dr. Charles Fay

The great thing about strong-willed, stubborn kids is that they give us quick feedback on our parenting prowess, or lack of it! Yep! As soon as our skills begin to slip, things get ugly.

Easy-going kids are another story. Unfortunately, they let us get away with far too many threats, lectures, reminders, warnings, unenforceable limits, etc. Because they're so sweet, it often takes far too long to realize when our parental behavior heads south.

Easy-going kids need Love and Logic, too. They need to make plenty of choices within limits. They need to make plenty of small mistakes. They need to own and solve their problems. They need to experience our empathy as they cope with consequences. They need all of these things, and much, much more, so that they have what it takes to survive in today's complex, oftentimes dangerous world.

The greatest danger for easy-going kids is that they won't make enough mistakes when they are young and the consequences of such mistakes are still small. We lose far too many sweet kids because their parents were tricked into using poor skills because of their sweet behavior.

Our CD, "Developing Character in Teens" provides a variety of strategies for helping kids ages five and up learn from safe mistakes rather than life-and-death ones. Don't wait until it's too late!

Thanks for reading!

Parenting Doesn't Need to Be a Lonely Job!
Dr. Charles Fay

Parenting kids can be a lonely job, particularly when they've got challenging behavior or special needs. Far too frequently parents of such children become progressively more isolated from the social support they need the very most. Many feel embarrassed by the problems they are facing. Others experience symptoms of withdrawal associated with anxiety, grief, and depression. Many find it difficult to meet others who can relate to their parenting struggles.

> *The more isolated we are as parents, the less effective we become.*

If you've slipped into this trap, there's hope! Are you aware that there are thousands of Love and Logic parenting groups through-out this country and abroad? Yes! Beginning in the 1980's, parents began to gather in these groups to learn how to parent their kids with Love and Logic. Since that time, the number of independent facilitators offering this service has increased to approximately 8,000 across the globe. While the primary purpose of these groups is to give specific parenting skills, a wonderful side-effect is the so-cial support of being in a group of parents who are struggling with the same issues. One woman put it well:

> *I loved the group, because it made me realize that I wasn't the only one in the world with kids who acted up!*

Give us a call at 1-800-338-4065, and we can help you get in touch with one of these facilitators, or get you on the road to be-come one yourself.

Thanks for reading!

Save Some Money
Jim Fay

Shirley and I spent our childrearing days strapped for money. Being young and uninformed, we tried to shield our kids from our trials and tribulations about getting the bills paid and keeping our credit rating up.

We thought we were doing the right thing. "As anxious as we are, we don't want them to worry. They're just kids and it's our job to manage the money," we agreed.

Years later, and a little wiser, we realized they would have probably felt more empowered had we made them part of the team and involved them in our strategy sessions. They could have been part of the problem-solving process.

Now with the sudden rise in gasoline and food prices we face the opportunity for many families to involve their kids in searching for ways to save some money.

This is a good time to share the family budget. Sit down with the kids and show them how you make up the budget and where the money has to go, saying, "Well, kids, since we are all in this together, where can we save some money? Do you have any ideas about how we can drive less, buy different kinds of food, or put off some purchases?"

You may be real surprised about the answers. And in some families parents may find out how spoiled their kids actually are.

Suggestion:

Have the kids help make up the grocery list. Put them in charge of policing your shopping, saying, "Okay, guys, which one of you is going to carry the list, check off the items, and make sure that I don't do any impulse buying?"

Here is a good and proper way for your kids to learn and to feel much more capable.

Thanks for reading!

School Uniforms

Dr. Charles Fay

Few things have stirred parental passions more than the prospect of mandatory school uniforms. Some believe they are too strict; that they stifle creativity and self-expression. I was one of those folks. Yep! Years ago I cringed at the idea of school children being forced to dress as clones. Something about it just rubbed my rebellious side wrong.

That was then.

After consulting with tens of thousands of highly effective educators in highly successful schools all over the world, I've completely changed my tune. My perspective on this subject gradually began to budge as I observed more and more schools enjoying the following benefits of mandatory uniforms:

- Students less distracted by competition over who's wearing the latest fashion or designer labels
- Students less distracted by scantily clad peers of the opposite sex
- Less bullying and teasing
- Fewer gang-related conflicts
- General improvement in student behavior
- Better teamwork among students and staff
- Happier kids

It's strange. When schools mandate student uniforms, people are upset at first, and tend to be a lot happier in the long run.

Thanks for reading!

....

Mom's Book Serves a New Purpose

Jim Fay

Mom left our conference with a new way of handling her kids, who routinely trashed the house, expecting her to clean up and prepare dinner while they were glued to the television.

She walked into the house with a book in hand, saying, "Wow, guys! What a mess. I'll start dinner as soon as it's cleaned up. I've got a great book I want to read. I'll be in my room reading. Let me know when the house is clean."

"No way, Mom! We have to eat right away. You have to drive us to our game this evening," they argued.

"Oh, guys. You worry too much," she answered as she headed to her room.

Her kids came into the room several times pleading with her to come out to fix dinner—without success.

Finally they sent the oldest in to say, "Mom. Are you on something? What have you been smoking?"

"Yeah, pal. I'm not on drugs if that's what you mean. But as you see, I've gone on strike. I'll no longer be your servant. If I don't take good care of myself, I don't know who will. Let me know when the house is clean."

She tells us that she keeps a book in her car. Each night as she arrives home from work she has it in her hand. When the kids see the book they yell, "Wait, Mom. The house is clean. Can you start dinner now?"

Mom is learning how to set limits, and her kids are learning how to be more responsible.

You can learn more about setting limits with our audio CD, *Love Me Enough To Set Some Limits*.

Thanks for reading.

....

My Kids Would Never Allow That
Jim Fay

I last wrote about a mother who went on strike. She was the one who returned home each day brandishing her book, heading for her room. She'd read until her kids had the house cleaned up. Only then would she cook dinner.

The results were so good that she told her friend, Melissa, about it. "Oh, my," worried Melissa. "My kids would never allow that!"

"WHAT? Her kids would never *allow* that," I thought. Has Melissa relinquished her parent ticket? Has she turned over family leadership and authority to her kids?

Is it possible that Melissa has bought into the fallacy that a parent's job is to make sure that kids are constantly happy? If so, her kids will grow up to be spoiled and entitled people who are frequently unhappy, believing they are victims whenever they don't get their way.

Parents who set reasonable limits often experience kids who are unhappy in the short term. It is natural for kids to be frustrated when they test limits and don't get their way. But this helps them turn out to be good people who are happy in the long term.

When parents do the right thing, it often feels wrong in the short term—especially when their kids throw a fit. But it usually turns out to be the best thing in the long term.

Learn more about how to avoid the disaster of entitlement in *From Innocence to Entitlement.*

Thanks for reading!

....

Internet Cautions
Dr. Charles Fay

With school back in full swing, most kids are spending time after school doing homework. Some of the homework may require the use of the computer and Internet. Although the Internet is a great resource, it must be used with caution. Dr. Charles Fay explains:

Good Kids Can Get in Trouble on the Web Too!

Plenty of adults have a hard time resisting the plethora of temptations provided by the Internet. You probably know one of these adults—or know their spouse, coworker, or boss. Many of them are bright and even well educated, but they've still fallen prey to online gambling, dating, pornography, shopping, etc.

If adults are struggling so much with these issues, don't for a minute believe that your kids won't too—even if they are "good" kids.

Many great and responsible young people have made mistakes that have got them into massive trouble on the Internet. That's why it's wise to never let your guard down when it comes to the sorts of things your youngsters are accessing. Listed below are some quick tips for keeping your kids, and yourself, safe:

- Don't allow them to have computers in their rooms.
- Regard the Internet as a very useful yet dangerous tool. Teach your kids that it's very similar to a chainsaw: useful in well-trained and mature hands, yet deadly in careless ones.
- Remember that it's your job as a parent to invade your kids' privacy. If you don't know what they are doing on the Web, you aren't doing your job.
- Remember that Love and Logic believes that kids should be allowed to make *affordable* mistakes. Chatting with pedophiles or ogling porn sites are NOT one of these.

For additional ideas on this topic, see our book, *Love and Logic Magic: When Kids Leave You Speechless.*

Thanks for reading!

Finishing the Race; and Enjoying It at the Same Time
Dr. Charles Fay

Have you ever met a "sprinter parent"? Like athletes competing for the gold in a fifty-yard dash, they throw every erg of their energy into trying to deal with each instance of misbehavior. Determined to raise great kids, they spend almost every moment trying to correct their youngsters' behavior.

Here's the problem: Parenting is a marathon—not a 50-yard dash! Those who start the journey as sprinters quickly run out of energy, get frustrated, and view parenting as painful.

135

"Marathon parents" know how to pick their battles. Because they know that parenting is a life-long task, they ask the following questions when they deal with misbehavior:

- Is this behavior dangerous in any way?
- If my child continued to do this for his entire life, would it *really* be a problem?
- Is this behavior a chronic problem?
- Is this a battle I can win right now without first getting support or ideas from others?

If the answer to these questions is "No," wise parents give themselves permission to rest, relax and reflect. By doing so, they preserve the energy needed to address problems with definite "Yes" answers. In our fun little book, *Love and Logicisms*, we provide 100 short parenting truths that help us determine the difference between the battles that must be won and those that don't need to be. Knowing the difference gives us the wisdom to finish the race and enjoy it at the same time.

Thanks for reading!

Don't Let Your Kids Play Divide and Conquer
Dr. Charles Fay

Since the beginning of time, kids have devoted themselves to the creative testing of parental limits. I suppose it's our job to set the limits, and it's their job to take them for a test drive. If they rev their motors, and our boundaries come crashing down, we're in big trouble—and so are they!

One common way they test our parental fortitude is by pitting us against each other. In families where there is marital tension, divorce, or remarriage, this type of testing can reach epic proportions. Maybe you've heard one of the following:

- Dad lets me!
- Mom said I could.
- Dad never listens. He's mean.
- Mom yelled at us!
- Why do you make me do that? Mom doesn't.
- Not fair. I'm telling Dad!

Resisting the urge to rescue your kids from the "mean" parent is critical! So is avoiding the trap of arguing with them about how you are right and the other parent is wrong. Wise parents stick to their limits and repeat with loving humor:

"Thanks for letting me know about that. Aren't you lucky to have parents who are different from each other?"

Kids don't need parents who are clones of each other. They do need parents who respect and support each other even when they don't agree about everything. For plenty of additional ideas on this issue, check out my new book, "Parenting Kids To Become the People Employers Really Want and…America Desperately Needs."

Thanks for reading!

Are you using too many words?
Dr. Charles Fay

Are you using too many words when things are going wrong with your kids? I struggle with this, too! There seems to be a part of my brain—the "lecture lobe," that occasionally takes over. Here's why this is a problem:

The more words we use when our kids are upset or acting out, the less effective we become. Every syllable just feeds the fire!

Why is this so? All kids crave attention and recognition from the adults in their lives. Extremely easy-going kids generally prefer the positive variety. In fact, they'll do just about anything to get it. In contrast, challenging children often get addicted to the negative, particularly when we fall into the habit of talking too much when they're acting out. Once this negative cycle gets started, they spend more and more time trying to push our buttons so that they can hear more exciting lectures laced with emotion.

To combat this sad state of affairs, Love and Logic parents remember the following:

Save the words for happy times!

In my CD, *"Oh Great! What do I do now?"* I provide a variety of Love and Logic alternatives to nagging, reminding or lecturing. All of these tools are designed to help you take better care of yourself while teaching your children that the best way to get your attention is to behave respectfully and responsibly.

Thanks for reading!

....

Chores at home = More success at school
Dr. Charles Fay

Is it difficult to get your kids to help around the house? Do you have to pay them to do the dishes, clean their room, etc? This week, Dr. Charles Fay provides some easy to use techniques to get your kids to do their chores without paying, begging, or bribing them.

Ask any veteran educator, and they'll agree:

Kids who are used to doing chores at home—without reminders, without pay, and without arguing—are far more respectful and motivated at school.

So, how's a parent actually get stubborn kids to do their fair share without resorting to begging, bribery, or full-scale warfare?

Listed below are some brief tips:

- When you see your kids working hard on a chore, offer to help them as long as they still work harder than you do. This rewards their hard work, gives you an opportunity to bond with them, and ups the odds that they'll be willing to help you when you are old and feeble.
- Give reasonable deadlines rather than saying, "Do it now!" Saying, "Just have it done by _____," has an added benefit: it gives you plenty of time to figure out what you will do if they refuse or forget to do the chore.
- Don't threaten, nag, remind, or warn. Just let them blow it.
- Do the chore for them.
- Lock in the empathy and expect them to repay you for your time by doing some of your chores, staying home instead of being driven somewhere, etc.

Learn more tips on this subject from our CD, *"Didn't I Tell You to Take Out the Trash?"*

Thanks for reading!

An Emotional Insurance Policy
Dr. Charles Fay

Being able to handle challenges life throws at you is something that must be learned. Unfortunately, many young adults have not learned how to handle those challenges. Read below for Dr. Charles Fay's advice on this matter.

Give Your Kids an Emotional Insurance Policy
The most fortunate folks on Earth have a strong voice in their hearts, reminding them that they have what it takes to make it through the tough times. Because they possess this "emotional insurance policy" they face life with optimism instead of anxiety.

139

They understand that the resources they have inside can never be taken away and will always be at their fingertips when needed.

One of the ways we give our kids this security is by giving them as many life skills as possible. In days gone by, most children learned these skills by being heavily involved in the family economy. They learned how to unplug pipes, nail nails, screw screws, cure leaking toilets, cook meals, clean clothes, and wash dishes by helping their parents.

In today's world, I find it quite sad: the vast number of bright young adults who know nothing about changing a tire, operating a washing machine, getting themselves unstuck from a snow bank, or using a phone book. People who lack these basic skills live lives completely dependent upon others, and lives full of anxiety. "What will I do if things go bad?" they wonder. "Who will take care of me?"

In my new book, "Parenting Kids to Become What Employers Really Want...And America Desperately Needs" (link to http://www.loveandlogic.com/ecom/pc-337-79-parenting-kids-to-become-the-people-employers-really-want-and-america-desperate-needs-sum.aspx), I share a variety of ways to give kids the gift of self-reliance. The first step involves making certain that they are learning along with you as you face life's daily challenges.

Thanks for reading!

....

Anger and Frustration Feed Misbehavior; Reminders Fuel Both
Dr. Charles Fay

Some kids are like solar panels. Instead of collecting their energy from sunlight, they gather theirs from the heat radiating off of our red faces. When we get frustrated and angry, they think, "Wow! How exciting! Let's try that one again!"

I struggle with this, too! Without thought, I start giving too many little reminders or warnings. Instead of simply enforcing limits when I'm still calm and collected, I let my lips flap until I'm nice and hot.

Bad idea!

When I remember to follow through without too many words, my kids behave better and so do I. For example, in our home we don't allow food outside of the kitchen or dining area. Since our two-year-old already knows this, there's no need for me to tell him again. When he breaks the rule, all I need to do is say, "Oh, how sad," and take the snack away. End of story.

When our 15-year-old doesn't do his chores, there's no need for discourse. All that's required is action. I can do his chores for him AND let him find out that I drive kids where they want to go when I'm not worn out from doing their chores.

In our new CD, *Keeping Cool When Parenting Heats Up*, you'll hear more ideas for parenting in a way that makes you proud.

Thanks for reading!

Stubborn Kids

Dr. Charles Fay

Have you ever noticed how strong-willed kids love to be told what to do? Yeah, they love it, because it gives them a chance to get stubborn and to show us who's really the boss! All that's required to achieve their goal is to do the opposite of what we want, do it extremely slowly, or develop a severe case of temporary hearing loss.

Here's a little experiment that might make your life a little easier with stubborn kids:

Put a smile on your face and replace telling with asking.

Instead of saying, "Pick up your toys," experiment with putting a smile on your face and asking, "What needs to be put away here?"

Instead of telling, "You need to take out the trash before we leave," experiment with a friendly, "What do you need to do before we can leave?"

Instead of, "Quit jumping on the couch," experiment with asking, "What did I say about being on the couch?"

Why do questions up the odds for cooperation? First, they stimulate thinking. The more pondering kids do, the less resistant they become. Questions also communicate, "You are so bright! You can figure this out!" I don't know about you, but I'm always better behaved around those wonderful people who make me feel this way.

For more ideas on staying sane around stubborn kids, listen to our CD, *Avoiding Power-Struggles with Kids*.

CHAPTER FIVE

For Educators

Tips for Win-Win Parent-Teacher Conferences
Dr. Charles Fay

I need to apologize—big time—to all of you educators! When we began these *Insider's Club* tips about two years ago, we got in the habit of providing parenting tips. While most of the ideas we've shared work just great in the classroom, we've neglected to address some of the tougher issues also faced by teachers. Our future goal is to share a nice mix of home and school strategies.

One of the toughest challenges faced by today's teachers involves working with Helicopter Parents. While they do it out of great love, these parents cripple their children by hovering over them and rescuing them from the consequences of their actions. Unwittingly, they also sabotage their children's learning by criticizing teachers for expecting too much out of their kids.

We've seen countless Helicopter Parents transformed by skillful, patient teachers. In his CD set *Putting Parents at Ease*, Jim Fay, my dad, teaches a variety of tips for building relationships with such parents so that everybody wins. Listed below is a sampling of these tips:

- Remember that parents who look angry and resistant are usually hurting inside.

- When we remember this, it becomes much easier to avoid becoming defensive or angry ourselves.
- The most powerful skill involves listening and allowing parents to vent about their frustrations before sharing our ideas.
- "Tell me more." "What would you like to see here?" or "How long have you felt this way?" are great responses to show parents how much you care and to get them talking.
- Share your ideas only after making sure that the parent is ready. Asking, "Would you like to hear my thoughts on this?" is a good way of showing respect and testing to see if they are ready to listen.

NOTE: These ideas also work great with angry spouses! Thanks for reading!

....

Chores in the Classroom
Dr. Charles Fay

The most successful teachers create a sense of family in their classroom. Some of them do this out of great gut-level instinct. Others understand the scientific research on human emotional needs. We all need to feel safe, to feel connected to a group, to feel needed, and to feel loved.

Student chores are an essential component of developing this sense of classroom family. One teacher commented:

Years ago, I discovered by accident, how important chores are. Because I was getting old and lazy, I decided to put my students to work on the tasks I didn't like doing. They all had jobs such as organizing the books, erasing the board, getting markers, throwing away junk that fell on the floor, etc. One day, a heated argument erupted between two of my tougher students. When I asked what was going on, one replied, "He's doing my job!"

In the book *Teaching With Love and Logic* Dave Funk comments on his own growth as a teacher:

I realized that every time I did something for kids that they could do for themselves, I was limiting them in the long run.

Chores aren't punishments! They're opportunities for students to feel great about themselves!

Thanks for reading!

....

Teaching Students to Listen
Dr. Charles Fay

There's nothing more frustrating than students who just won't listen and follow instructions! In every classroom, there seem to be at least one or two. To make matters worse, their selective hearing impairment seems contagious.

How do successful teachers, and parents, train kids to listen? Listed below are some suggestions:

Build special relationships with your most resistant students. Great teachers know that tough students are far more likely to listen to teachers they love.

Set limits only for things over which you have total control. Unsuccessful teachers and parents are famous for attempting to set limits on things they could never control in a million years. Successful teachers use Enforceable Statements to set limits.

Great teachers say things like, "I give full credit to papers handed in on time." Less successful teachers say, "Hand your papers in on time."

Enforce limits without repeated warnings and reminders. Effective parents and teachers remember that kids will always come to need at least the same number of warnings and reminders they are given.

For additional ideas on building cooperative teacher-student relationships, applying Enforceable Statements in the classroom, and managing behavior as you teach, listen to our CD, *Quick and Easy Classroom Interventions.*

Thanks for reading!

....

Swearing Student Proves No Sweat for Love and Logic Teacher

Dr. Charles Fay

I was recently blessed to hear a wonderful story—a tale of a teacher using Love and Logic with a student who called her a vulgar name. Although shocked and hurt, her Love and Logic training paid off. "Ohhhh, this is not good," she replied. "You must be having a rough day. We'll talk about this later."

Perplexed by her calm response, the student grunted, "Huh?"

He was escorted to the office where he awaited his fate. "This is between you and your teacher," the principal told him. "She'll visit with you after school. Your mom will pick you up afterwards."

During their meeting, the teacher described some options for solving the problem. These included meeting with the school resource officer and paying a fine for disorderly conduct, in-school suspension, or helping her with "community service" tasks around the school.

He opted for helping her out. After working with her for two weeks, he realized that she really wasn't what he'd called her. They developed a positive relationship, and there was no more name calling that year!

The teacher learned these skills when her school offered our *Nine Essential Skills for the Love and Logic Classroom* teacher training curriculum. You can give the gift of these skills to your staff,

146

too! Although this curriculum requires no additional training to teach, those who attend our conference October 23-25 will get "insider information" that will dramatically increase their success. This will be a very special event limited to no more than 175 participants. Don't wait to register!

Thanks for reading!

CHAPTER SIX

Special Topics

Do Kids With ADHD Need Reminders?

Dr. Charles Fay

A question we're often asked goes something like the following:

Is it really fair to expect children with ADHD to do things like chores, get ready for school in the morning, and finish their homework without frequent reminders?

If we want children to need frequent reminders, we should give them.

If we're more interested in creating kids with the capacity to become self-sufficient, responsible and proud, it's much wiser to teach them "self-reminding" skills and hold them accountable for using these skills.

Can you teach your child how to make and follow checklists?

Can you take pictures of your child completing the different tasks required to get ready in the morning? Wouldn't life be better for you, and your child, if she learned to use these as guide?

Is your child capable of keeping and using a written date book or electronic organizer?

Can you do these things instead of crippling a child with reminders?

Thanks for reading!

Helping Kids Cope with the Loss of a Loved One
Dr. Charles Fay

There's nothing tougher to deal with than the loss of a loved one. During these difficult times, many parents turn to Love and Logic for answers about how to help their kids cope. Listed below are some tips:

Honesty is usually the best policy. When we give our kids honest, age-appropriate information, it sends the message that they can handle such information.

Remember that kids take their emotional cues from us. When they see us handling the loss by allowing ourselves to cry, talk about our sadness, and do healthy things to move on with our lives, the odds go way up that they will do the same.

Do more listening than talking. Probably the biggest mistake made by well-meaning parents involves trying to take away the child's pain. As strange as it may sound, when we listen to their pain, and allow them to have it, they get through it much faster.

For more practical tips for helping kids cope, listen to the CD, *Childhood Grief and Loss,* by Foster W. Cline, M.D.

Thanks for reading!

....

No More "No!"
Foster W. Cline, M.D.

By the time Jacob was three, he had heard the word 'No!' about 15,000 times! And, according to some research, that number is low. So when Jacob's mom said, "It's time to take your medicine," what do you think he said? You guessed it! The problem is, this wasn't just your typical toddler control battle. Jacob needs his medication to stay alive, because he has cystic fibrosis.

Jacob's mom, unknowingly, had trained him to say 'no.' In fact, she trained him really well! *Wise parents learn early on to say 'no' as much as necessary but as little as possible.* So when can parents safely 'just say no'?

1. When children are young and parents can easily enforce the limits they set.
2. When children respect and love parents enough to do what they ask them to do.
3. When children are older, if consequences will do the teaching if they don't 'abide by the no.'

So what about little Jacob? His mom learned how to set limits without saying 'no' by using just a couple of Love and Logic techniques like choices and enforceable statements. I am happy to report that Jacob is now enjoying good health and a great relationship with his dear mom.

This tip was taken from Love and Logic's newest book *Parenting Children with Health Issues* by Foster W. Cline, MD and Lisa Greene.

....

Can ADHD Kids Behave?
Dr. Charles Fay

Q: Can kids with ADHD really learn, remember, and behave?
A: ABSOLUTELY!

Q: What's the secret?
A: Use the very same techniques proven effective with kids who don't have ADHD.

Q: Are you kidding?
A: No! Here's why. Children with ADHD have the very same be-

haviors as children who don't have ADHD. They just display them far more frequently and intensely. For example, all kids fail to pay attention from time to time, forget what we ask them to do, argue, occasionally misbehave in impulsive ways, and experience bouts of excessive activity, etc.

Q: So, will Love and Logic work with my child with ADHD?
A: Yes! In our CD, "Calming the Chaos of ADHD" we teach how to match the high frequency and intensity of their challenging behavior with a high frequency and intensity of Love and Logic techniques.

Q: So there's hope?
A: Yes! As long as you don't get tricked into believing that they're incapable of learning and behaving.

Thanks for reading!

The Challenge for Kids with Talent
Dr. Charles Fay

Some of the brattiest kids I've ever met have been ones endowed with special gifts from birth. Why? Early in the lives, the adults around them became so enamored by their special talents that they let them get away with sin!

Academically gifted kids are far too frequently allowed to argue and negotiate about how the home or classroom should be run. Athletically gifted kids are too often allowed to break all sorts of rules without being held accountable. Extremely attractive children often learn that they can get their way if they cast the right little look.

The sturdiest homes crumble when built on foundations of sand. Such is the case when we become so distracted by our children's gifts that we make excuses for their misbehavior. The world is filled with gifted people who live lives of misery. Why? Because they were never expected to struggle for anything, they were always allowed to run the show, and they were rarely held accountable for the problems they created. Just one glance at the lives of many Hollywood "elite" illustrates this point in vivid detail.

Thanks for wanting more for your talented children!

Adult Limits
Dr. Charles Fay

I'm very lucky. Both of my parents behave pretty darn well.

Some folks aren't so lucky. Their parents spend much of the time criticizing their choice of careers, their spouses, their parenting, and just about everything else they do.

If you're reading this tip, I'm sure that you love your kids enough to set and enforce limits. Do you also love yourself enough to set limits with the adults you love?

Listed below are some limits that I've seen healthy adults set with their parents:

- It's hard for me to visit when you put down_____. I'll visit you when I don't feel criticized.
- Feel free to come by as long as I don't have to hear about how bad you think that my _____is.
- I really love you too much to spend all of our time together arguing about_____.

Adults tend to be just like kids. When we set limits, they get mad in the short term and tend to behave better in the long term. Check out our book on marriage, and see how this applies to spouses!

Thanks for reading!

Will Love and Logic Work With Autistic Children?
Dr. Charles Fay

Just about everywhere I travel, someone asks me if Love and Logic will work with a child having a diagnosis of "autism-spectrum" disorder. Because this diagnosis is applied to so many different types of children with very differing abilities and needs, it's difficult to provide a blanket "Yes" or "No" answer.

Here are some things we do know about Autism and Love and Logic:

- It's not uncommon to hear people say that Love and Logic has changed their lives with their autistic child.
- They relate that remaining calm, using empathy, and being careful to avoid using lectures or threats helps their children avoid meltdowns.
- Most of them also tell us that, although their children are capable of learning, they require a lot more teaching and practice—and empathy—to learn basic social and behavioral skills such as taking turns, waiting, staying seated, following directions, etc.
- Visual cues really seem to help these kids. Many parents find it helpful to take pictures of specific tasks and use these pictures to prompt their children.
- The people who are the most successful are those who experiment with the Love and Logic skills, modify them a slight bit to fit their specific situation, and stop using the ones that don't seem to work.

In his book, *Love and Logic for Children with Special Needs*, Dave Funk provides an inspiring look at how children with autism and other special needs can learn, achieve, and feel good about themselves.

How has Love and Logic worked with the autistic child in your life? Send us your story at cservice@loveandlogic.com.

Thanks for reading!

Divorce: Helping Your Kids Cope
Dr. Charles Fay

If you've ever gone through a divorce, you certainly don't need anyone to tell you how painful and confusing it can be! Although I'm certainly not proud to admit it, I've been there. After years of reflection on my own experience, as well as work with many other families navigating this pain, I humbly offer four small tips for helping kids cope:

- **Remember that they need to feel free to love both of you.**
  During the pain of a divorce, it's awfully tempting to talk negatively about one's ex. It's also very easy to send a variety of powerful nonverbal messages that indicate to your kids that they will be disloyal to you for loving the other parent. The damage this does to children is immense and long-term.

- **Understand that the healthier you grieve, the healthier they will.**
  Parents who get stuck in anger inevitably act in ways that alienate their children from the other parent, and from themselves. Parents who work through their grief with help from friends, family, faith family members, and professionals are far less likely to fall into this trap.

- **Resist the urge to parent through guilt.**
  Wise parents keep the end goal in sight. This goal—to create respectful and responsible adults—helps them remain firm even when their kids say things like, "But Dad lets me!"

- **Listen, listen, listen, and empathize.**
  Our kids need to know that it's okay and very natural to be upset about the entire ordeal as long as they are not acting in disrespectful or irresponsible ways.

For more tips on helping kids cope with grief of all types, listen to *Grief, Trauma, Loss: Helping Kids Cope*, by Foster W. Cline, M.D. Thanks for reading!

155

About the Authors

CHARLES FAY, PH.D.

Charles Fay, Ph.D. is a parent, author and consultant to schools, parent groups and mental health professionals around the world. His expertise in developing and teaching practical discipline strategies has been refined through work with severely disturbed youth in school, hospital and community settings. Charles has developed an acute understanding of the most challenging students. Having grown up with Love and Logic, he also provides a unique...and often humorous...perspective.

JIM FAY

Jim Fay is one of America's most sought-after presenters and authors in the area of parenting and school discipline. His background includes 31 years as a teacher and administrator, over three decades as a professional consultant, and many years as the parent of three children. Jim's sense of humor and infectious spirit have made his interviews, audios, videos, and books popular with educators and parents as well as the national news media. Jim has discovered that fun stories are the most powerful way of helping people learn. He often comments, "People seem to learn best when they giggle." You will find this delightful quality in many of our Love and Logic products.

DAVE FUNK

Dave Funk has been an educator since 1969 and has taught in both regular and special education classrooms. He is responsible for participating in the evaluation and placement of disabled students, coordinating a number of special programs, and serving as liaison to parent groups. Dave has participated in numerous conferences as a sectional presenter and keynote speaker. In addition, he is the co-author, with Jim Fay, of *Teaching with Love and Logic*, and the author of *Love and Logic Solutions for Kids with Special Needs*.

FOSTER W. CLINE, M.D.

Dr. Cline, a nationally recognized psychiatrist, is co-founder of the Cline/Fay Institute, Inc. He is a favorite consultant to psychiatric institutes, schools, and parent groups. His writings are the source of many revolutionary approaches to dealing with childhood problems. Foster is known for his ability to provide creative, effective solutions for behavior problems. His presentations are lively and humorous, while providing practical techniques that produce immediate results. His most recent book, *Parenting Children with Health Issues: Essential Tools, Tips and Tactics for Raising Kids with Chronic Illness, Medical Conditions and Special Healthcare Needs* is now available.

Index

A

abuse
  helping kids understand the cycle
    of, 53–54
  parental, 74
accountability, 126
acting out, 105
action, taking, 57
ADHD, 97
  and behaving, 151–152
  and learning, 151–152
  and reminders, 149
  teaching kids self-reminder
    skills, 149
advertising
  as misleading to kids, 48
ages seven to twelve, 23–40
aggressive kids
  principles for helping, 55
  tendencies of, 54–55
alcohol, 41. *See also* drinking alcohol
allowance, 102
  automatic allowance withdrawals, 24
  for clothing, 42
  wasting, 126

Anderson, Larry, 73
anger, 5, 58, 91, 115, 141
  and homework, 25
  and parents, 105
  and youth, 54–55
  avoiding, 10
Angry and Oppositional Students
    (CD), 55
apologies
forced, 89–90
when you do not need to give, 100
    appreciation, 65
arguing
  avoiding the trap of, 137
by kids 35, 47
with your kids, 44, 80, 94, 95, 116
attention
  being the center of, 108
  children trying to get, 88–89
  giving less, 17
  giving more, 34
autism, 154
Avoiding Power Struggles With Kids, 29,
    124, 142
"Awe, man," 71

toys, 6
    donating, 11–12
    tantrums over, 8
transitions
    to school, 32–33
trash, taking out
    steps for making it happen, 127–128
trust card defense, 48
    when children have something to
      hide, 48

U
Uh-Oh song, 2, 4, 5, 6, 12, 16
underachievement, by kids, 121
uniforms, school, 132
    benefits of, 132

V
victims, of bullying, 33–34
video games, 105, 124
    limiting, 33, 121
voice, silent
    power of, 2
volunteering, by kids, 33

W
warnings, 129
"What a bummer," 62, 71, 81, 94, 119
"What did I say?" 116
wisdom
    from making bad decisions, 96
    to make good decisions, 95
words
    naughty, 28
    saving for happy times, 1
    using fewer, 17, 76
    using too many, 137–138
Words Will Never Hurt Me, 33
work
    having pride in, 127
    never working harder than your
      kids, 23, 25, 104, 118